THE 50 BEST WAYS TO
simplify your life

PROVEN TECHNIQUES FOR
ACHIEVING LASTING BALANCE

PATRICK FANNING & HEATHER GARNOS MITCHENER

New Harbinger Publications, Inc.

Publisher's Note

Distributed in the U.S.A. by Publishers Group West; in Canada by Raincoast Books; in Great Britain by Airlift Book Company, Ltd.; in South Africa by Real Books, Ltd.; in Australia by Boobook; and in New Zealand by Tandem Press.

Copyright © 2001 by Patrick Fanning and Heather Garnos Mitchener
New Harbinger Publications, Inc.
5674 Shattuck Avenue
Oakland, CA 94609

Cover design by Amy Shoup
Cover photo by Gladys/Photonica
Edited by Clancy Drake
Book design by Michele Waters

Library of Congress number: 01-132284
ISBN 1-57224-255-8 Paperback

New Harbinger Publications' Web site address: www.newharbinger.com

02

10   9   8   7   6   5   4   3

For Nancy
—P. F.

For Kris
—H. G. M.

contents

CONTENTS   CONTENTS   CONTENTS   CONTENTS
CONTENTS   CONTENTS   CONTENTS   CONTENTS   CONTENTS
CONTENTS   CONTENTS   CONTENTS   CONTENTS   CONTENTS
CONTENTS   CONTENTS   CONTENTS   CONTENTS

RELATIONSHIPS   71

SPIRIT   91

FURTHER READING   113

INTRODUCTION **introduction** INTRODUCTION
INTRODUCTION INTRODUCTION INTRODUCTION INTRODUCTION
INTRODUCTION INTRODUCTION INTRODUCTION INTRODUCTION
INTRODUCTION INTRODUCTION INTRODUCTION ✠

1. Find Your Balance

Simplicity is not a state of rest. It's a dynamic, ever changing balancing act that occurs on several continuums: financial, business, relationships, kids, spirituality, you name it. With so many life elements to juggle, you will need to look at each one separately and evaluate its importance to you. Only then will you understand how to make these disparate elements work together to create the life you want to live. It will most likely take some experimenting to find your balance, which is where this book can help.

The goal is not to arrive at a static balance point in your life—which is impossible anyway—but to become skilled at the dynamic process of shifting the center point so that the whole asymmetrical structure of your life remains in balance. This kind of balance is like that of a mobile. If there's too much physical or emotional or financial stuff occupying your time and your mind, you can't keep the whole structure in sight and in balance. Though it may not come crashing down on you, it feels like it's going to, which is where the problem lies. At the very least, the mobile will lack harmony and elegance, and you'll lack the time and energy to appreciate whatever beauty there is in your life. To begin restoring the mobile to harmony, map out your life's elements so you can see how they all hang together at this point in time.

Gather several large pieces of paper and colored pens or pencils. Sit and think for a little while about how you would map your life and all its categories. Be sure to include not just the areas that currently demand your attention but also those that you may be neglecting. An essential part of finding your balance is filling in any gaps. Remember, as you simplify certain areas of your life, other areas will have room to expand. So make sure to include anything that you've been interested in but haven't had time to explore.

As to the physical form of this exploration, just see what develops. You might decide to use symbols, the spokes of a wheel, a pie chart, a bar graph, circles of various sizes, or a simple list. You can use color to differentiate between the different areas. If you find you can't bring it to life with just pen and paper, add photos or other materials. You can even build a mobile out of elements that symbolize the various parts of your life. Let your mind puzzle it out to your satisfaction. It may take a few tries to put your thoughts into a form that makes sense, so don't rush yourself.

After your initial attempt, put the results away for a few days, and continue to think about your delicate balancing act. Then come back to your life map with a fresh perspective. You may realize that you left out a very important part. Or maybe you don't feel right about allowing a certain aspect to occupy such a big portion of your time. Perhaps something you thought you could minimize is tugging at your mind, looking for more attention. Add to or revise your creation as necessary.

Keep your map handy as you read this book, and modify it as you adapt our ideas to your own unique life and its challenges.

2. Unravel the Myth of Voluntary Simplicity

Do you find simplicity very complicated? If so, you're not crazy. You have a good grasp on reality and you're in good company.

The term "voluntary simplicity" was coined by Richard Gregg in a 1936 essay about Mahatma Gandhi's efforts to revitalize rural India's tradition of cottage industry. In 1981 Duane Elgin adopted the term as the title of his classic book, *Voluntary Simplicity*. Elgin took Gandhi's socioeconomic ideal and gave it an ecological spin: "In an interdependent, ecologically conscious world every aspect of life will be touched and changed: consumption levels and patterns, living and working environments, political attitudes and processes, international ethics and relations, the uses of mass media, education, and many more."

In many ways, Elgin describes a way of life that is *not* simpler, but actually *more complex* than what it replaces. Here are just a few obvious examples of how this is so:

Simple	Complex
Dump all the trash into one can	Sort the recyclables
Just buy stuff	Study each manufacturer's ethics
Jump in the car and go	Take the bus or ride your bike
Microwave a frozen pizza	Cook whole foods from scratch
Turn on the TV	Read aloud to your child
Buy supermarket produce	Grow an organic garden

The "simplicity" in "voluntary simplicity" is mythical for two reasons. First, as the above comparison shows, many "simple" lifestyle choices like recycling or carpooling are actually more complex and time-consuming than the behaviors they replace. Second, these more sustainable lifestyle choices often don't really replace old patterns—they are added on top of old patterns, making for more complex lives, not simpler ones. For example, you may have switched to buying most things with cash to avoid running up credit card bills, but you still need at least one credit card for things like hotel reservations and renting cars when you travel. Cooking more meals at home with fresh ingredients will not free you from having to own and maintain a refrigerator. If you decide to grow an organic garden, you can add gardening tools, canning equipment, and perhaps a freezer to your possessions. No matter how much you take the bus, ride your bike, and carpool, you are still probably stuck with owning and maintaining a car as well.

Elgin's ecologically conscious world is an ideal vision, like Utopia or Shangri La. Such visions typically tout their own "simplicity" and ease while downplaying their complexity and difficulty. Many of Elgin's predictions of society's growing commitment to sustainable living have come true. Recycling is a growing industry. Construction, manufacturing, and mining have become more earth-friendly. But we don't live in Utopia yet.

So don't feel like a failure if you find voluntary simplicity very complicated and exhausting. It *is* complicated and it *does* take energy. Do the "simple" things because they are more satisfying and enriching, and don't expect them to be really simple. And when you're too tired or busy to be simple, give yourself a guilt-free break and order the pizza.

3. Hold on to Your Passion

With all you're giving up, there's one thing you'd better keep hold of: your passion. You'll need it. When you start saying no to materialism, cutting your expenses, and lowering your standard of living, some people will have negative reactions ranging from gentle teasing to outright hostility. Why? Because they'll be upset and worried and threatened.

Your friends may have visions of you peering down snootily at them from your lofty moral perch. Your spouse might fear you're going to drag him or her off to die miserably in an unheated shack in the woods. Your parents, so proud of your myriad accomplishments, could start to think you're slacking off. And the kids will probably think you've suddenly gone hippie on them. If you get these reactions, it may be because others see your interest in simplifying as a challenge to their own lifestyles: What do you mean, you're going to spend less money and buy fewer things, and still end up with a higher quality of life? What do you mean, you're going to simplify your relationships and pay more attention to your inner life? What makes you so special? You'll have to have some passion to stay on track. Of course this is your life, not theirs. But that doesn't mean it's easy to listen to the criticisms and doubts of the people you care about most.

Although you may be suffering slings and arrows, try to be sensitive and positive when you're talking to others about the changes you've made and are continuing to make. It's great to share your ideas and enthusiasm with others; if you do that, you stand a decent chance of inspiring them to make similar changes. Just take care not to judge anyone else's lifestyle, even indirectly, by talking disparagingly about your own former habits (such as mentioning how *stupid* you used to be about this, or how you can't believe you *ever* did that). Whether or not others are content with their life, your passing judgment won't help convince them that you're right—and it may even turn them against your ideas. Just because your own life felt like a disaster area not so long ago doesn't mean that it's okay to lecture people, even those who seem to be setting themselves up for a breakdown. They need to independently reach the same conclusion that you did: that it's time to simplify for their *own* sakes.

So how do you retain your passion in the face of opposition? First, think back on the aggravations that led you to seek out simplification in the first place: too much time in the car, too many credit card payments, the effects of persistent neglect on your worn-out body. Remember that whatever prompted you to change is something you're glad to leave behind. Keep that in sight when you come up against opposition. Just as you don't know what's right for him, the other guy doesn't know what's right for you—it's for you to decide.

Next, keep reminding yourself of the goals you've already achieved, whatever they may be: more free time to explore your needs, increased interaction with friends and family, freedom from possession obsession, streamlined finances, a peaceful home.

Finally, lean on the people in your life who *do* support your effort. A little positive feedback from a few like-minded souls can do a lot to counteract the naysaying of the skeptics. And if you keep your level of passion high enough, it's likely that the ranks of your supporters will keep on growing.

HOME HOME HOME HOME **home** HOME HOME
HOME HOME HOME HOME HOME HOME HOME HOME
HOME HOME HOME HOME HOME HOME HOME HOME HOME
HOME HOME HOME HOME HOME HOME HOME ✦

4. Create a Haven

Turning your home into a place of peace and simplicity is a worthwhile goal with big rewards. All it requires is a willingness to embrace your individuality and make up your own mind about what you want your home to be, in both a physical and an emotional sense.

Start with an easy mental exercise. Close your eyes and visualize the elements that epitomize your ideal simple home. Once you have a picture in your mind, open your eyes and put your ideas down on paper. Be as general or as specific as you like: imagine an organized linen closet, a quiet corner with a comfy chair and the perfect reading lamp, time alone in the house one evening a week, less time spent doing chores, spiritual shelter from the world and all its chaos, a home office with a place for everything, a spalike bathroom. You have to know what you need before you can start to bring it about, so take the time to get your vision right.

Using your wish list, start figuring out what steps you can realistically take to create a simple haven that lives up to your ideals. Formulate these steps in terms of the time, money, and energy you have to spend. Don't be surprised if it turns out to be difficult to keep a balance between the resources you can use and the payoff you expect. We live in a culture of planned obsolescence, where we're expected and encouraged to care about the latest and greatest window treatments and the hipness quotient of the bathroom color scheme. This is where your individuality and a little introspection come in. Do you honestly care about the opinions of Madison Avenue, those lifestyle gurus, and the couple next door?

You can get clues about what works for your life not only from the times you followed a trend and regretted it later, but also from the times you resisted the cultural pull and felt good about it—like the six-week backpacking trip you took in lieu of new carpeting.

So, with your resources, personal style, and goals firmly in mind, take a look at the dream list you made. Where do you most want to spend your resources? Which items can be accomplished with time and ingenuity rather than money? Whose help do you need to make these changes a reality? To free up resources, can you stop spending time and money on things you don't care about?

A few guidelines:

- It doesn't simplify your life to embark on a project you can't finish. Be realistic about how much of a do-it-yourselfer you really are. Ask for (or hire) help if you need it.

- If a change requires piles of money or an unreasonable imposition on other people, ask yourself whether it's really a simplifier after all.

- Consider whether you actually need to buy anything to accomplish your goals. If you're working on an organizational challenge, for example, you might be able to fashion a solution from things you already have on hand (see #5, Get Organized).

- Don't feel pressured to solve "problems" that don't bother you. Maybe you don't care about setting up your library alphabetically, but you'd happily devote a couple of weekends to creating a home office setup or making your living room feel cozier. Put your time and energy where it matters to you.

- For serenity's sake, consider a serious decluttering effort. That means not holding onto things just because they might come in handy someday. Paring down to what's truly useful or treasured can completely change the way you view your home and your possessions.

5. Get Organized

Getting organized requires only two things: a little time and a lot of determination. A bonus is that along the way, you'll be able to clear out your clutter, if you haven't done so already. In fact, decluttering should be part of the process: after all, who wants to sort and organize a bunch of stuff they never use? (See #4, Create a Haven, and #7, Convert Clutter to Cash, for inspiration.) You'll also get some insights into habits and routines that may be frustrating you and wasting your time.

One hint that helps: resolve to rein in your household purchasing at least until you know what you already have squirreled away in the nooks and crannies of your home. Most likely you'll be surprised by how much stuff you own that you've entirely forgotten about! In fact, as tempting as it may be to run out and buy some nifty (and perhaps overpriced) storage units, caddies, and bins, wait until you've decluttered, sorted, and assessed your storage needs. Then, staying in your simple mindset, consider whether you already have something in which to store these items. Shoe boxes, plastic food storage containers with lids, zippered cosmetics bags—all these can work just as well for your storage needs as a new setup from the ContainerVille superstore. If you must buy organizing aids, wait until you know for sure how much space you have for them, and how much stuff needs to fit into them. The containers should fit your belongings, not the other way around.

Begin by sizing up your problem areas and making a plan of attack. Where to start? If you're easily discouraged, start with a small, confined area like a single drawer. Otherwise, target the area that gives you the most grief. As an example, we'll talk about that ubiquitous catchall, the hall closet. The closet we have in mind has so much stuff in it that we go there first to look for things we can't find, thinking they must be there. It's so full, in fact, that we risk head injury every time we open the door.

First, we carve out an appropriate chunk of time—from fifteen minutes to a whole day, depending on the size of the task. Our closet is looking like quite a job. It's a small space, but it's packed to the gills. So we set aside two hours for sorting and assessment, and we assume we'll need to figure out some new storage solutions too, bringing the total to about four hours. Next, we gather a few cardboard boxes and take them to the work area, designating them for different categories of belongings: things that belong here; things that have strayed from their intended place or never had a place; things to discard, give away, or sell; and things to repair or refurbish.

As we remove each item from the closet, we ask, "Do I want or need to keep this?" If the answer is no, it gets sorted into the appropriate box. If the answer is yes, the next question is whether the item belongs in this area. If not, we place it in the "belongs elsewhere" box. If so, we put it in the keeper box—but we don't leave it in the closet, because we want to empty that space out completely and assess what needs to fit back in. We repeat the process with all the items, until we're looking at an empty space that turns out to be bigger than we originally thought. Turning our attention to the keepers that belong here, we group like items together. The categories we come up with for our closet are outerwear, umbrellas, frequently used sports equipment, bike repair tools, and the vacuum cleaner. These items merit space here because we grab them on the way out the door or we use them very often. Now, how to fit them into the space? Umbrellas go into a tall metal wastebasket, leaving more hooks for the coats—so each family member gets a spot of his or her own. Several pairs of running shoes and one pair of in-line skates go into a large plastic bin, keeping them out of the way so the vacuum cleaner can slide freely in and out. The bike repair tools, formerly scattered on a shelf, are zipped into an old cosmetics travel bag, leaving room for a basket full of winter hats, a set of knee and elbow pads, and two helmets.

These basic principles of sorting and grouping belongings make it simple to get organized. And provided you don't reclutter your life, keeping it organized is simple too.

6. Contemplate the Three C's

Modern life runs on cars, computers, and credit—the three Cs. To thrive today, you should have a good car and take care of it, a good computer and know how to use it, and good credit that you keep under control.

Some gurus of simplicity look to the third world for a model of the simple life, concluding that you should sell your car and computer and cut up your credit cards. Unfortunately, what is simplicity in Nigeria is often disability in the United States. Without a car you may be essentially immobilized. Without computer access you are cut off from an increasingly important mode of community discourse. And lack of a credit card (and the credit history it brings) limits your economic power.

Cars

When you strip cars of the glamour of their advertising and the horror of their impact on the environment, you are left with a handful of truisms that go back to the dawn of the automotive age:

- New cars are more reliable than used ones, but they cost too much, so a late model, low mileage used car is a better deal.

- Fixing your old car is always cheaper than replacing it with a comparable car.

- Learning how your car works and maintaining it properly mean it won't be such a hassle: check fluids, belts, and hoses frequently; change the oil every 5,000 miles; and replace worn, weak, frayed, leaky parts *before* you break down.

- A car is a device to get from point A to point B, not a sex toy or an enemy.

Computers

At different times in history, electric lights, air travel, automobiles, and telephones were widely considered to be insidious, dangerous intrusions of a demonic technology that would destroy life as we know it. Somehow we survived, and we will survive the computerization of modern life. Whether you are a computer addict or a technophobe, it's time to come to terms with the hallmark device of the twenty-first century. The truisms about cars also apply to computers, with some revisions:

- The new models are faster than your old computer, but they cost too much.

- Upgrading your old computer is cheaper than buying a new one.

- Learning how your computer works and maintaining it properly mean it won't be such a hassle. Save your work and back up your files frequently.

- A computer is a device to communicate, research, and create, not a sex toy, a drug, or an enemy.

Credit

The wisdom of living within your means is timeless. As Dickens' Mr. Micawber explained it to David Copperfield, "Annual income twenty pounds, annual expenditure nineteen nineteen and six, result happiness. Annual income twenty pounds, annual expenditure twenty pounds ought and six, result misery."

The world economy is built on credit and debt, with endless buy-now-pay-later mechanisms such as student loans, installment plans, mortgages, credit cards, stock margin accounts, lines of credit, and so on. There are countless ways to go into debt and only three ways to get out: bankruptcy, death, or paying it back.

If you are currently burdened by credit card debt, simplifying your life will involve paying it back, which is as simple as it is painful:

- Track all your income and expenditures.

- Maximize income and cut expenses to the bone.

- Make a budget that allows as large a debt payment as possible every payday.

- Pay off high-interest debt first.

- Stick to the plan until you are debt free. Thereafter, keep only one credit card, use it sparingly, and pay it down to zero every month.

7. Convert Clutter to Cash

Would your life be simpler if you just had less stuff? Consider holding a garage sale to transform unwanted stuff into a form that is easier to store: money.

Drive around next weekend and scope out your local garage sales. Don't take any money. Check out asking prices for stuff that is comparable to yours. Talk to the people holding the sales and ask them where they advertised their sale. Notice the importance of big, clear signs, a good location with lots of traffic, and ample, safe parking.

If you don't have a good location, find somebody who does and wants to cohost a garage sale with you. Make sure they know that your priority is to get rid of stuff, not make a fortune. If you can't find a partner, maybe there's a local flea market where you can rent some space. Set the date, giving yourself several weeks to get ready.

Start stocking the store early. Go through every room in your house or apartment, every drawer and closet and cupboard. Pull out anything that you haven't used in the last eighteen months and throw it in the corner for the garage sale. Soon every room will have a corner full of stuff that is cluttering up your life, stuff you'd be better off without.

Stifle any negative thoughts like, "But that was a wedding present … I paid 800 bucks for that … I could wear that again if I lost weight … Maybe cousin Jim could use that … It's too good to sell ... That has sentimental value." You do not have to find the perfect disposition for every thumbtack in your collection. Remember that your goal is to get rid of clutter, not to torture yourself with guilt, regret, and indecision.

Price everything over $10 ahead of time. Set prices low and plan to come down even further. Encourage quantity purchases by sorting small stuff like books, toys, dishes, and utensils into boxes marked "$1 each, 3 for $2, 10 for $5," etc. Plan to have a table heaped with nearly worthless stuff for sale like this: "$5 for all you can fit in a grocery bag." Sell ordinary clothes like shirts and blouses like this as well.

In the week before the event, call the newspaper and put in your classified ad (make sure you get it in by the deadline—call early to find out when that is). Make signs—big, high contrast, simple, and clear. Make sure you have the staple gun or wire or tape you need to put them up Friday night. (Don't wait until Saturday morning—you won't have time.) Gather change, cash box, grocery bags, folding tables, clothes racks, and so on.

At last it's Saturday morning. The early birds will descend to cherry-pick the merchandise. Smile and let them. If someone thinks your bottom price is too high, offer to throw in another item free—do whatever it takes to move stuff out. As the day goes on, avoid complex deals involving deposits to hold items for pickup next Wednesday. Sell everything cash and carry, this weekend only.

At the end of the sale, *don't put anything back in your home*. No matter what's left, take it straight to the Goodwill or whatever nonprofit is open Sunday evenings for just this purpose. Beware of the temptation to "save it for the next garage sale." If you think that, you are in danger of becoming a garage sale junkie. That way lies more clutter, not less.

So put the money in your pocket, wave goodbye to the leftovers, and go inside to your roomy, uncluttered home.

8. Revise Your Routines

We all love and need our routines: they're comforting, and they give a structure and format to the day. But are all your routines working in your favor, supporting your desire for a simpler life? Here are just a few areas where you may be able to streamline.

Wardrobe

One of two opposite approaches can work here, depending on your personality. Clare sticks to a basic color palette so that her clothes can easily be mixed and matched. She buys individual items in one of those favorite colors—and knows she already has something that goes with it. Julie, on the other hand, has varied tastes and likes to keep up with current trends, so she doesn't want to limit herself to timeless basics. Instead, she has a hard-and-fast rule that she never buys separates; when she finds a piece she really wants, she won't buy it unless she can complete the outfit on that same shopping trip. Both women know what styles flatter them, so they don't waste time or money on items that they'll never wear. Another trick is to keep only the items that you really love. Better to have half as much stuff in the closet—but all of it wearable.

Grooming

If you're not sure you need to simplify your grooming routine, think about how much time you spend on it every morning and evening, as well as how much time and money you spend on appointments for professional services like haircuts and manicures. Are there other things you'd rather be doing with your time and your hard-earned cash? If so, consider first whether any of the services you have done professionally can be done at home instead. That's a big money-saver, and it eliminates the need to fit appointments into your schedule as well. At the least, consider a haircut that is easy for you to maintain and style so that you don't have to spend too much time on your hair each day. When it comes to makeup, less really is more. Figure out which basics you can't live without, and stick to the brands and colors that you know work for you. If you want to keep up with trends, all you need to do is update your lipstick color every so often. Another thing to keep tabs on is the number of grooming products you use daily. With the cleansers, potions, and lotions involved in bathing and caring for skin, hair, and contact lenses, a person can easily end up with well over a dozen products. And as your overcrowded bathroom shelves may attest, every item you use requires storage and regular replacement. Luckily, many products today do double duty, and it's well worth experimenting with these to see if you can lighten your load and speed up your routine.

Housework

Many of us have emotional baggage about the way our homes look. Unexpressed feelings about our jobs and relationships can translate into obsessive cleaning or total neglect. And our ideas about what's "good enough" are often based on the ideals put forth in TV commercials—you know, that kitchen floor that's clean enough to serve as an operating table. On the practical side, getting straight on who's responsible for what is a good start toward streamlining your housecleaning activities. If you share a home with family members or friends, figure out a division of labor that seems fair to all concerned. If you have kids, don't forget to include them in the chores. Though it seems to be less common than in previous generations for children to have regular chores, doing a few things around the house didn't hurt *you*, did it? Whether you live alone or with others, it's important to determine which chores give a result that really matters to you. Devote more of your cleaning time to those, and modify the others as you see fit. Regularity also helps, because if you keep up with moderate amounts of cleaning, your place won't get so filthy that you have to devote whole days at a time to cleaning it. And when you do get overwhelmed, remember this: as you simplify your life and eliminate clutter, cleaning will get much easier.

9. Slow the Flow

Just too much. Those three little words probably resonate with you, or you wouldn't be reading this book. Too much to do, too much information, too much *stuff*. Here are just a few ways to reduce the flow and make space in your world for the things that really count.

Information

Do you feel you have to keep up with every bit of news? If you do it because you love it, then great. But if you do it out of obligation, decide instead which subjects excite you the most. Maybe you can't live without a dose of local politics. Perhaps you crave news from countries that don't get much attention in the press. Or you might want to know every single move Congress makes. Whatever your passion, seek it out, and let the rest of the data out there flow past you. Are you overloaded with visual and audio stimulation? Consider leaving the TV and radio off for a change. See what it feels like to experience your own thoughts and ideas, rather than what the media wants to feed you. Are you constantly tied to the Internet, looking at news updates? Do you receive multiple e-mail newsletters? Go ahead and unsubscribe. Billions of pieces of information are out there for the taking, and you can find them later if you want them. In all, be selective in giving your attention to the media. Despite how it may seem sometimes, there's no law that says you have to take it all in.

Paper

How many magazines and newspapers do you subscribe to? And how many do you actually read and enjoy? Consider dumping those subscriptions that you renew only out of habit. Resist picking up "free" publications unless you truly intend to read them. Plagued by junk mail? You can drastically reduce the amount of junk mail you receive by following the advice in the booklet *Stop Junk Mail Forever* by Marc

Eisenson (see Further Reading section). In the meantime, toss these useless items into the recycling bin *without* letting them distract you. Rest assured, nothing earthshaking has happened in the home furnishings arena in the ten days since you received the last catalog. When you check your mail, keep only the bills and the correspondence from actual humans. The humans you know don't send any correspondence, you say? Try writing to them—they just might be inspired to write back.

Stuff

This is a difficult one. Before you pick up something off the store shelf, before you accept a hand-me-down item from a friend "just in case" you might need it someday, before you engage in your next online or sale-at-the-mall spree, ask yourself these questions:

1. Do I really need it?

2. How often will I use it?

3. Where will I store it?

4. Is there a fantastic reason why I can't just walk away?

If asking yourself these questions doesn't help you reduce your purchases, then you either already have a pared-down, simple approach to possessions, or you need to try another trick. Carry a slip of paper in your wallet on which you keep a wish list. When you see something you really want, write the date, item, store, and price on the wish list. After a month, take a look at the items on the list. Do you remember why you were so eager to buy those shoes, that gadget, this set of kitchen chairs? Do you still salivate at the thought of the purchase, or does the idea leave you cold now that you're not in merchandise mania mode? Chances are you won't even remember why the item seemed so necessary at the time.

10. Hire It Out

Who says you have to do the simplifying thing single-handedly? In addition to getting your family and friends on the bandwagon, you may wish to bring in a hired gun for particular problem areas.

Try as he might, Stan wasn't able to reduce his work hours and still keep the job he loved. But he hated coming home to his messy apartment after a long day at work, and wished he had more hours in the day. He toyed with the idea of hiring a housecleaner, but it didn't feel right to him because all his friends seemed to manage on their own. Why couldn't he? One night a woman he'd been dating dropped by unannounced, but Stan was too embarrassed to invite her in. At last he was ready to get help. He hired someone to come in once a week and do the big jobs, leaving just the basic tidying-up to him. Now he was free to enjoy Saturdays with friends without feeling guilty that another weekend would pass without housecleaning. To make up for the extra expense of the cleaning, he substituted some dinners out with dinner parties in his newly tidy apartment. Instead of fretting about how his place looked, he spent the day of a dinner party working on his Italian cooking skills with an expert friend.

Elisabeth loved working in her garden, growing vegetables and flowers. As a gardener and all-around outdoorsperson, she felt duty-bound to do all the lawn care too, even though she hated it. A friend finally convinced her to hire a neighborhood kid to do it, and Elisabeth used the free time to experiment with grafting fruit trees, a process that had long intrigued her. The new varieties she grew also inspired her to expand her culinary repertoire.

You may be able to think of an area where hiring someone—for a one-time-only gig or an ongoing task—would make a big difference in your life. Start by making a list of routine chores around the house and yard. Next, write down the big jobs that only have to be done a few times a year. Include everything you can think of that really must get done on a regular or semiregular basis.

Now take an honest look at your list. Which routine chores do you always skip over? Do they build up to the point where an easy task becomes a bona fide pain in the neck? Would getting those things done by someone else take a load off your mind? How about those big items: spring cleaning, window washing, finally taking that pile of stuff in the basement to the dump? You may keep pushing these tasks away year after year. There may even be items you didn't think of putting on your list because you don't think of them as chores. Do you end up dining out a lot or ordering takeout because you hate going grocery shopping? Do you fear doing your own taxes but struggle through it anyway, because it seems you should be able to handle it? Maybe you've made many failed attempts to get your home or office organized, and you could use a day of consultation with a professional.

Be honest with yourself here. No one knows your life the way you do. Set aside your guilty feelings about what you "should" do—because sometimes the way to simplify is to delegate. (For the flip side of this perspective, see #29, Practice Self-Reliance.)

11. Change Your Culinary Attitude

Simplifying the process of preparing meals probably doesn't require a complete revolution in your habits—although we can't promise that, since we've never had dinner at your house. Here are a few ideas that should help you put good food on the table even when the rest of your life feels too complicated.

A Simpler Diet

- Learn to enjoy the fresh taste of less-processed foods that are lower in fat and sodium.
- Choose seasonal ingredients when possible. Try your local farmers' market.
- Buy ingredients that work in a variety of dishes.
- Make big batches of the foods you love and freeze extra servings for later. Or just cook a little extra so you have enough for lunch the next day.

Above all, realize that a meal doesn't always have to be a big production to be good and good for you. Instead of popping another frozen entrée in the microwave, bake some potatoes and top them with chopped veggies, herbs, and a grating of cheese. Or have a bowl of oatmeal, or a scrambled egg and toast made with good whole-grain bread: just because it's too complicated to cook breakfast foods in the morning doesn't mean you can't enjoy them at other times of the day. (For more thoughts on a simpler diet, see #44, Feed Your Soul.)

Family Cookbook

Because we live in a time of unprecedented abundance, many of us spend a lot of time trying to decide what we want to eat. We may not spend as much time obtaining food as did our hunter-gatherer ancestors, but we're not getting any exercise out of the deal either. To help combat the "I don't know, what do *you* want?" syndrome, try compiling a simple family cookbook.

Start with a list of the meals that you know and love (or at least like). Concentrate on those that are relatively easy to prepare and that all members of the household are willing to eat. Then, every time you try a new recipe that you like, add it to the list. If the recipe is from a cookbook, list the book and the page number. If it's from a newspaper or magazine, clip it out *right away* and attach it to the list (saving old newspapers will *not* simplify your life!). The family cookbook can be a great way to expand your repertoire and get new dishes into a regular rotation. Simple doesn't have to mean boring.

Inspect Your Gadgets ...

... and decide how many of them are actually doing you any good. If you walked into your kitchen right now and opened the drawers and cupboards, how many of your tools and gadgets could you immediately identify? And of those, how many have you used in the past year? Do you find yourself pushing aside useless, overly specialized dealie-bobs to find the items you use every week, like the measuring cups and cheese grater? A couple of sharp knives, well cared for, can take the place of a lot of gadgets.

When it comes to electrical gizmos for food preparation, consider whether it's really more efficient to use the item when you take into account the hassle of hauling it out of its storage nook, setting it up, and then cleaning it up. If not, seriously consider getting rid of it.

12. Take a TV Time-out

You love television; you hate television. It's a waste of time; it's the only activity you have the energy for sometimes. It's boring and insipid; it's soothing and calming and asks nothing of you. The kids can't seem to stay away, losing interest in other activities, but you're tempted to let the situation stand because it seems so much easier than making a change.

Beth, a corporate lawyer who combined long workdays with an active social life, came home exhausted most nights. She crashed in front of the TV, sometimes falling asleep with it droning away. While Beth depended on her TV ritual to help her wind down, increasingly she found that it left her feeling restless and aggravated. The constant parade of perfect-looking people and luxury goods contributed to a sense that her life was inadequate. But it was hard to break the habit in favor of a more fulfilling pursuit.

Bob and Marie, academics who value reading and conversation, were both on departmental committees that required occasional evening meetings and social events. As their schedules got busier, it seemed so simple to let their sons Jordan and Jeff, ages nine and eleven, watch a bit more TV than they did before. Pretty soon the kids were begging for an expensive game console and the games to go with it, and they were caught up in the quest for certain collectible pieces of plastic junk, which were immediately forgotten and abandoned under the sofa for the dog to find and chew up. Jordan, formerly so excited about baseball practice and his shot at shortstop, seemed to wish he were home on the couch instead of on the field.

You may see yourself in these situations. Or maybe you're the mom at home with an infant, sick of having the talk shows in the background of your life, tired of turning to the tube in your rare "free" moments—between feedings and laundry and vacuuming—instead of finally picking up that new novel you've been dying to read. Or you're one half of a couple in a serious rut: dinner in front of the TV, followed by chips and ice cream also in front of the TV. What happened to music and conversation or a quiet stroll around the block after dinner?

We seem to invite this box of tubes and wires into our lives not so much because we really want it, but because it's always been there and seems necessary if we're to stay in touch with the world. So what's the solution? This one really *is* simple: turn the thing off, and leave it off, at least for a while. You'll be surprised at how little you miss it. Beth took up stretching as her new winding-down ritual—something she'd long wanted to do. She even dusted off her neglected but beloved CD collection and played some of her old favorites while stretching away her stresses. As a side benefit, she found she slept better without the sensationalism of the TV news intruding on her thoughts.

Those of you who want to wean your kids off TV have a tougher row to hoe. The youngsters may not be eager to take up watercolor painting, engage in stimulating conversation, or practice meditation. However, any time you can shift from TV-watching to more physically and mentally stimulating activities will benefit your kids in the long run. Make a plan that seems realistic, fair, and in keeping with your values. For many families, that means allowing a fixed amount of TV-watching; for others it means getting rid of the TV entirely, despite objections from the kids. Bob and Marie took a moderate approach. They let each of the boys choose their favorite shows to watch, and limited TV time to those shows. They scaled back their committee activities slightly to allow themselves more time to play games with the boys, even instituting a family "poker night"—sans cigars and beer—and making it a weekly ritual. Your family might choose crafts or art projects, language study, or playing musical instruments together.

WORK WORK WORK WORK **work** WORK WORK WORK
WORK WORK WORK WORK WORK WORK WORK WORK WORK
WORK WORK WORK WORK WORK WORK WORK WORK WORK
WORK WORK WORK WORK WORK WORK WORK

13. Calculate Your True Hourly Wage

Regina worked at a computer fifty hours a week formatting catalog pages for a mail order company. She considered herself lucky to have steady work at $15 an hour, since she had never finished college and had few marketable skills. But she was crabby and tired and her wrists hurt despite the carpal braces. She wanted to spend more time with her husband, maybe have a baby before she was too old. But how could they manage without her full-time salary?

The answer came when she figured out her true hourly wage. She estimated all the time and money she spent each week in order to keep working at her job, including hidden money and time robbers like unwinding after work and shopping for work clothes:

	Dollars per week	Hours per week
Commuting (bridge tolls, gas)	$10	7
Shopping for and cleaning work clothes	21	1
Lunches and coffee	49	5
Unwinding after work	–	7
Work-related illness	18	3
Vacations to recharge	46	2
Housekeeper	35	1
Unpaid overtime	–	10
Total	**$179**	**36 hours**

Regina spent $179 of her own money and thirty-six hours of her own time in order to hold down her full-time job. When she added the extra hours and subtracted the costs, she discovered that it took her seventy-six hours each week to net $421. Divided by seventy-six hours, that $421 gave her a true hourly wage of only $5.54.

Her eyes were opened. No way was she going to ruin her wrists, starve her relationship with her husband, and become a childless divorcee for a measly $5.54 an hour. She realized that she could actually afford to cut back to twenty hours of work a week, if she could do it at home on her own computer. By doing her own housework, cooking meals at home, not commuting, wearing sweats instead of silk, and taking cheaper local vacations, she could make enough money to live comfortably and get her life back.

The concept of calculating your true hourly wage is simple, but the process might take you a while. Consider these questions:

1. If you didn't have your job, how would you spend your time and money differently?

2. What dues and insurance premiums would you not have to pay?

3. How much time and money do you spend commuting to work?

4. What toll does work take on your health, and how could you express it in terms of time and money?

5. What job-related clothes or tools or training do you have to pay for?

6. In order to hold down your job, how much do you spend on child care, yard work, maid service, restaurant lunches, cappuccino, gym memberships, business gifts, taxis, parking, wireless phone bills, coworker birthdays, or bar tabs?

7. How much more take-home, disposable cash would you have if you dropped into the next lower tax bracket?

8. If your job provides medical coverage, what is it worth on an hourly basis? How much could you cut your weekly hours and still be covered? Or what would it cost you to pay premiums yourself?

Regina found that she felt better physically when she worked fewer hours. Her wrists stopped aching and she had more stamina. She had time and energy enough to take a night class, working toward finishing her degree. She and her husband started talking seriously about having a baby.

14. Get off the Clock

Nothing complicates your life like a full-time job, unless it's a full-time job with lots of overtime. When you are stuck at your computer terminal or on the phone or in the company car for forty or fifty hours a week, you don't have much time and energy left over for simplifying your life.

And it's not like time at work is quality time. A lot of workplace time is wasted in gossiping, socializing, and conspiring, or filled with meetings, redundant and pointless committees, task forces with nothing to do, housekeeping functions, and low priority, routine tasks.

The "80/20 rule" is a truism in studies of workplace productivity: 80 percent of the work is done by 20 percent of the people. The most important 80 percent of the average worker's tasks are accomplished in 20 percent of the work week. Time and again it is shown that 80 percent of the results come from 20 percent of the effort. The trick is to increase your productivity so that you are the one who is getting 80 percent of the results in 20 percent of the time (and not the other way around!). Then figure out *how to get paid for your results, not for your time.*

How could this be arranged? The simplest and best solution is to escape the office. Can you talk your boss into letting you work at home and telecommute by phone, fax, and e-mail? Many people find that in three hours of concentrated work at home they accomplish what would take them eight hours in the office, with all its distractions and interruptions. This means they can finish their day's work by 11:30 and have the rest of the day off with pay.

When Jeanie's boss at the real estate office gave her a huge project of compiling a mailing list of all newcomers to the county, she convinced him that she could do it faster and more accurately at home on her own computer. Two days a week she worked at home, putting in about half-time. She finished the project early, and drummed up other special home projects that allowed her to escape the office about half the time. She did the average "day's" work from nine to midnight, after the kids were in bed.

If you can't work at home, try to cut down to part-time as a way to escape time spent at work. Make up for the lost income by practicing some of the money saving tips in this book, or by spending your extra free time doing things for yourself that you used to pay for. Roy is an accountant and his wife May is a nurse. They both limit their work to twenty-five hours a week—just enough to live modestly but well and qualify for health benefits.

A more drastic way to escape the office is to just quit. Give up your salaried position and become a freelancer or consultant, performing for several companies that special 20 percent of your old job that you do so well and so efficiently. Roz worked for years for a weekly newspaper, writing copy, selling ads, and setting type. When the paper was bought out by a big chain, Roz downsized herself into an independent contractor. She charged twice her old hourly rate, and had time left over to pick up work from three other weeklies in the area.

Jeanie, Roy, May, and Roz all know the secret of balancing private life and work life by getting off the clock, capitalizing on their special expertise and interests, and getting paid for results, not time in harness.

15. Explore Right Livelihood

Right livelihood is a Buddhist ideal summed up in the 1960s admonition to be "part of the solution, not part of the problem." If you are a vegetarian pacifist, you'll be happier if you quit your job at the slaughterhouse, turn down the position at the napalm factory, and become a social worker or open a health food store.

Right livelihood simplifies your life by giving you a mission. When your profession matches your values, your self-esteem rises and you can more easily weather complication, disappointment, and stress. You're also less likely to feel greed and envy in response to TV advertising or the financial prosperity of others.

To find your right livelihood, ask yourself these questions:

- What do I do for fun?
- What do I avoid?
- Whom do I admire?
- Whom do I hate?
- What inspires me?
- What disgusts me?

Carol was a music major whose answers were that she enjoyed playing flute and piano and avoided history and math. She admired musicians and classical composers and hated snobby, self-important people. She was inspired by her ensemble performance instructor and disgusted by the pulp mill that made her hometown stink and poisoned the river.

After school, Carol felt she had to make some real money to pay off student loans and get ahead in life. She worked for three miserable years at an insurance company in Omaha, where she didn't like the people or the work, didn't have enough time for her music, and felt like a failure despite the decent salary she was earning. Her life became simpler and happier when she moved back to her hometown and found her right livelihood: teaching band in the middle school, giving piano lessons on the side, and volunteering at a pollution watchdog group.

Right livelihood is not something you figure out once and for all at age twenty-five. It's a lifelong process of growth and reevaluation. Carol married the school principal and had three daughters. Her values shifted to encompass motherhood, early Renaissance music, and a deeper understanding of watershed ecology. She directed all the musical events at her daughters' schools. She quit teaching band, started performing with a local recorder quartet, and began teaching a woodwind ensemble class at the junior college. She took biology classes and dragged her kids up and down the local creeks on monitoring and restoration projects.

As people live longer and the average retirement age recedes to seventy and beyond, many must find a second or third right livelihood. The passions and professions of youth no longer satisfy the way they did thirty years ago. When Carol's youngest daughter went away to college, she quit teaching music and took a job with the local water quality control board, a bureaucracy that she used to consider the enemy. Despite her early hatred of math and history, Carol had become very good at using computers to keep track of time, money, and information. She computerized the water board's files, helping ensure that wastewater monitoring and inspections happened on time.

Eventually Carol was appointed to the water board's board of directors as a citizen member. She still played music, but mostly pickup sessions with old friends and Christmas carols for her grandchildren. She never made a big salary, but she followed her heart to her right livelihoods.

16. Get a Day Planner (and Use It)

Sometimes poor time management makes life seem more complicated than it really is. Better planning can reduce the stress a busy schedule brings. Fortunately, business consultants and calendar manufacturers have been perfecting the technology of time and task management for the past fifty years. Visit an office supply store and pick up one of the many day planner products available.

Look for a simple calendar, small enough to carry with you at all times, that shows a day or a week at a time. The same system will work for work and personal commitments. Most will be set up in some form of "T Scheduling," a two-column format that looks like the following entry from Dave's planner:

Saturday, April 7, 2001

Get tax form from library—A3	8-10	9:30 Jenny soccer—A1
Lawn mower to shop—B2	10-12	
Take down Christmas lights—C2	12-2	
Memo to Fred and Mabel—B1	2-4	1-5 P.M. toxics drop-off—C1
Return video—B3	4-6	
Van estimate—A2	6-8	7:00 potluck, scout hall, dessert—B4
Mail Scott's summer camp form—A4	8-10	

The column on the left contains things Dave has been planning to do sometime on Saturday. The column on the right is for appointments and other time-sensitive tasks. It's a busy day, and writing it down like this helps him get it all done. Dave sees that he can get up by 7:30, wash Jenny's soccer jersey, get Scott's summer camp form finished and ready to mail, load the video, the car insurance papers, and the lawn mower in the van, and jot down the number of the income tax form he needs.

Then at 9:00 he can take Jenny to her soccer game and watch it until 10:00, when the library, the video store, and the body shop are open and he can pick up the tax form, return the video, and get an estimate to fix the dents from the accident he had in January. He'll swing by the field for the end of the game, mail the camp form, and go home for lunch. It will take him two hours to clean out all the old paint and solvent cans in the garage and back porch and schlep them over to the toxics drop-off depot at the community center. On the way back he can pick up a pie for the potluck. He can work on the memo to Fred and Mabel for a while, then leave for the potluck. By the time he's back home, it will be too dark to take down the Christmas lights, but heck, they've been up since December, so what's another week?

If you start writing down everything you want to get done, you'll soon see that it's impossible to accomplish every task, every day. You need to prioritize. The most common way to prioritize is the A-B-C, 1-2-3 method Dave used. Go quickly down your list of tasks and give every one a letter grade:

A   Absolutely essential, must be done today

B   Pretty important, but less so than A

C   Relatively minor, could wait a while

Then go back and rank the A items 1, 2, 3, and so on in order of importance. Then do the same for the B items, starting over at 1, then rank the C items. On Dave's list, you can see how he ranked his tasks. The idea is simple and powerful: get the most important stuff done first and the less important stuff done second, and let the least important stuff slide if you have to. (For a discussion of how to work personal passions into a too-tight schedule, see #42, Create an Acronym All Your Own.)

17. Give Perfectionism the Boot

How can doing things perfectly complicate your work life? It's hard to see the harm in doing things well, but there *is* a difference—a big one—between high standards and perfectionistic beliefs. The trouble comes when you cross that line. Unrealistic ideas about yourself and your work can make it hard for you to get through your workday in one piece, let alone simplify it.

So how do you know if you've stepped past high standards and into perfectionism? Ask yourself whether you engage in any of the following perfectionistic behaviors:

- Excessive checking of work; not knowing when to quit
- Repeating or correcting your work or that of others
- Constantly seeking reassurance from your coworkers or supervisor
- Spending so much time on organizing that your actual work suffers
- Difficulty making decisions
- Trouble meeting deadlines; slowness
- Giving up too soon due to anxiety
- Avoiding tasks because you fear you'll be inadequate

Fighting these tendencies will do more than make your workday more efficient (and hopefully shorter). You'll also avoid the negative feelings brought on when perfectionistic standards are not met, including worry, a feeling of being overwhelmed, and a lack of spontaneity—or even anger, anxiety, depression, or obsessive-compulsive behaviors.

One particularly insidious aspect of perfectionism in the workplace is that it can affect much more than just the way you do your own work. If your unrealistic standards interfere with what other people are trying to do, you may wreak havoc on your work relationships. Thinking that people "should" do things a certain way and trying to control them just adds another category of tasks to your workday—tasks that others would probably prefer to see you drop from your list! Micromanaging people or projects won't endear you to anyone, and it does nothing but complicate your life. And if you're a supervisor who applies impossibly high standards to your employees and acts angry, intolerant, and critical when they quite naturally fall short, you will most likely have to spend time dealing with high employee turnover.

After pinpointing the behaviors that may be getting in your way, consider whether some of the following thought patterns are contributing:

- Do you doubt yourself and your abilities?

- Do you think mistakes are equivalent to failure?

- Do you fail to see the bigger picture?

- Do you focus on negative details and ignore positive ones?

- Do you worry excessively about getting others' approval?

- Do you inappropriately compare yourself to others?

- Do you think in terms of how things "should" be?

- Do you try to control people and situations?

In addition to recognizing the irrationality of these unrealistic beliefs and working to loosen their control over your behaviors, keep an eye out for people and activities that trigger your perfectionism. Workplace patterns tend to be pretty well established, so once you figure out your problem areas, you'll know where to direct your efforts. If you have trouble understanding the hold irrational beliefs have over you and need help conquering them, *Prisoners of Belief* by Matthew McKay and Patrick Fanning is a very helpful tool.

18. Learn to Focus

For most of us, the pace of the modern workday contributes to a feeling that life is much too complicated. We're expected to shift gears constantly, which can leave us feeling frazzled and overwhelmed. Even though we take pride in multitasking, and despite the fact that it's often considered an asset in an employee, this habit doesn't always serve us well. But when we're bombarded with e-mail, ringing phones, and colleagues popping in, how else are we supposed to function? Is it really possible to stop bouncing around and learn to focus when there's so much going on?

You may have already discovered that simplifying your life allows you to focus on the things that matter most to you. Conversely, focusing on the important things at work will simplify your workday. A few easy techniques will help you.

Start by prioritizing your tasks for the day. If you don't have a grasp on what you have to do, it's hard to know where to direct the laser beam of your attention. In ranking your tasks, try to balance your desire to check items off your list with the knowledge that the tougher jobs should sometimes take precedence. (Include blocks of time to deal with your e-mail and phone calls.) Make sure to tackle jobs *before* they hit the emergency stage—otherwise you'll be forced to put out fires when it might not be convenient or efficient. Next, estimate how long each task will take, or in the case of a longer-term project, how much time you can realistically devote to it today. Check your calendar for any meetings or other events that will break up your day. That way you won't schedule a one-hour job twenty minutes before the mandatory staff meeting. Last, fit the jobs you want to do today into the available time.

Now that you know what you're doing and in what order, try these tips to help you zero in on the task at hand:

Get Free of Distractions

- Check e-mail at set times, rather than letting each new message interrupt you.

- Set aside a time to retrieve voice mail and return calls.

- If possible, turn off your cell phone (especially if you use it mainly for personal calls).

- Try working on difficult projects early or late in the day, depending on when your workplace is quieter. If your office empties out at noon, if you have the freedom to do so.

- Don't be afraid to let others know you'd like not to be disturbed for a set amount of time.

Structure Your Work

- If you don't keep a calendar of your deadlines and obligations, start now—it's essential if you hope to stay focused and in charge of your day.

- For each project, no matter how small, make sure you have everything you need before you start.

- Schedule breaks for yourself. Knowing that a break is coming up makes it easier to stay on course.

- Try to find a stopping point at day's end that allows you to walk out the door at peace. If you can, give five minutes' thought to your priorities for tomorrow.

- Last but not least, revel in your growing sense of accomplishment.

19. Do It Now!

Sure, everything needs to be done now. Pronto. ASAP. Hop to it! The boss is waiting! Clients are waiting! But you can't do *everything* right now, you say? True, but you can do *some* things now. Yes, we're talking about putting an end to that old bugaboo that causes so much of the rush-rush of our daily lives: procrastination. You can really simplify your work life if you stop putting things off.

To beat procrastination, you first need to figure out why you do it. Fear is a big reason. Other times, it's that the task seems so unpleasant that you just can't face it. Or maybe you have so much work piled up on your desk that you simply don't know where to start.

If fear is what gets you, set about figuring out what you're afraid of: Doing a less-than-perfect job? Letting your colleagues see that behind your iron shield of competence is a confused mess of a human being? Asking for advice about something you feel you should know inside and out? Most of these fears would seem pretty irrational if you really thought about them. But they can still influence your behavior. Next, think about how these fears add up to a much bigger fear: procrastinating so long that you fail to do the project at all. Can you see how the smaller fears actually contribute to the bigger, more serious fear coming true? Even if your self-preservation instinct kicks in and you manage to tackle the fearsome task before the deadline whizzes past, you may find that the act of procrastinating has led to the realization of your original fears: you rush through your work, making mistakes that you wouldn't have made if you'd given yourself sufficient time, or you end up asking coworkers to cover for you so you can skip a meeting and work on an overdue report instead.

If facing up to an unpleasant task gets you every time, the solution is both easy and difficult. It's easy because there's a very simple solution: do the unpleasant thing first! It's difficult because no one wants to do yucky tasks—that's why you're in this pickle in the first place. So a change of mind is really what's in order here. Putting off unpleasant chores complicates things in two ways: you feel guilt for not doing what you're supposed to do, and dread because you always have it hanging over your head. Worse still, the task will get tougher the longer you put it off. That famously irritable customer won't start acting nice if you avoid calling him back for two days; the tax board will only make things tougher for you if your quarterly filing is late; turning in the department budget two weeks after the due date means that your boss takes flak from her boss (which comes right back to you). To turn your avoidance tendency around, try to look down the line and visualize the even *more* unpleasant things you'll avoid by doing that tiresome task right now.

If you put things off simply because you don't know where to start, then it's time to get organized. Knowing where things are, when they are due, and what needs to be done to complete them is essential to keeping your work on track and on time. To figure out what works for people in your industry, ask your better-organized colleagues for tips. For general organizational skills, there are dozens of helpful books on the market. If you truly feel you are hopeless (or that you will procrastinate about tackling your organizational difficulties), then hire a consultant—today!

A bonus: beating procrastination will simplify your personal life too.

20. Handle It Once and for All

Here's a basic trick that many well-organized people rely on: whenever possible, handle your correspondence and other paperwork just once. To see how this tip helps simplify your work life, think about how many times the average piece of paper passes through your hands before you really deal with it.

You pick it up from your mail slot, or someone puts it on your chair to make sure you see it. You look at it briefly, then add it to the stack in your In box. When it looks like the tower might be ready to tumble, you scan through it, sorting the stack into topical piles to be dealt with later. Maybe you even clip parts of the stack together. At this point you might get rid of things you don't need—the junk mail, catalogs, etc. Or maybe you don't. Maybe you think, oh, I'll look at that while I eat lunch today. The stacks to be dealt with get set aside. More stacks are placed on top of those stacks. Everything's going swimmingly until Amy stops by to ask whether you've read that copy yet, and if you haven't, then could you please do it today? Hey, no problem, since you sorta kinda read it two days ago, but you just didn't know where to go to check the spelling of that guy's name. So you had set it aside to do later, and now you just have to find it in one of the stacks. Get the picture? If this is familiar, you're not alone. And the solution is easy: quit sorting and resorting that same darn stack of paper.

The simple trick to handling most papers only once is to set aside time each day to deal with them. You'll read or scan each item and do one of the following:

- Throw it away (and figure out how to stop getting it if it's junk).

- File it.

- Reply to it.

- Delegate it.

- Schedule it to be completed by a specific date, if it's too big to take care of now.

See how easy it is? We recommend doing this at the same time each day—first thing in the morning, the last hour before you go home, right after lunch, whatever works for you. After you've been doing it for a while, it will go more quickly. You'll know what to junk immediately and what to take care of right away. And you will have figured out how to stop getting those items you don't want or need. Best of all, you'll never have to sort through another mountain of paper again. (See #9, Slow the Flow, for more tips.)

As you can see, this exercise connects to procrastination, time management, organization, focusing, and many other themes of this book. As you practice handling papers only once, you may be alerted to problem areas that you can try to improve upon to further simplify your life.

21. Maximize the Positive

The activities that were described in #14, Get Off the Clock, as having such a negative impact on your time management at work—like gossiping, complaining, and backbiting—have other, more internal effects as well. They may amplify your feelings of anxiety, anger, or frustration about your job. By putting an emphasis on the positive at work, you can immediately increase the amount of serenity and calmness in your day. Over the long term, you're more likely to be satisfied with the meaning of your work and your purpose in life.

Fresh out of school, Jack was thrilled to find the exact opening he'd imagined: a position as an assistant at a public relations firm representing nonprofit groups. Eager to work, he jumped in with both feet. At first it was great, but after about six months he noticed that he and his fellow assistants spent what seemed like hours every day complaining about certain coworkers, speculating about the motives of one particular upper-level manager, and just generally whining about deadlines and other work demands. Sometimes he got so riled up that he found himself getting irritated with his clients, even when they asked him for routine assistance.

The continuing negativity started to wear on Jack, so he asked himself how he felt about the job. The truthful answer was that he loved it. He liked his manager and almost all of his coworkers, and he felt gratified when he helped his clients achieve their goals. So what was all the complaining about then? All he could figure out was that it was just an accepted part of corporate culture—everyone could relate to the little gripes and annoyances of workaday life, and it seemed to give most of them a "we're all in the same boat here" kind of camaraderie. But Jack wasn't deriving comfort from that part of the culture. All the griping was starting to warp his perspective of the work, and it was even beginning to make it seem like he was in the wrong place, when at bottom he liked the place quite well.

So what to do about it? He decided to gradually distance himself from the negative parts of the work chat. The easiest thing to do was to stop instigating bitch sessions, which he sometimes did out of habit. That was the first step. Next he practiced tuning out other people's negative comments and refusing to let them sweep him along. Finally, once he got used to looking at things in a more positive light, he found he could tactfully avert a negative conversation by telling an amusing story or starting a discussion of something non–work-related. Two years later, he still looks forward to coming to work each day, and he enjoys his friendships with coworkers and his good relationship with his supervisor. His life has not become unnecessarily complicated with negative feelings about his job, and he has grown in it. When he looks back at what he's achieved so far and imagines how others envision him, he's especially glad that he made the changes he did.

If you're in a similar situation at work, as so many of us are, there are a number of steps you can take:

- If you are more stressed out by your interactions with people than by the work itself, try to identify your trigger situations and devise alternate behaviors you can use when those situations arise. Take note of whether you tend to instigate the negative behavior or simply follow along.

- Try to figure out why you indulge in the gossip or complaining: boredom, anxiety, insecurity, and a need to connect are all common reasons. Recognizing the underlying emotions will help you change your patterns.

- Practice viewing your coworkers and clients as partners rather than adversaries.

- Whenever possible, introduce new topics of conversation as a way to bond with your coworkers. Give people a chance to show other sides of themselves, and you'll learn things that may surprise and delight you.

MONEY MONEY MONEY MONEY **money** MONEY
MONEY MONEY MONEY MONEY MONEY MONEY MONEY MONEY
MONEY MONEY MONEY MONEY MONEY MONEY MONEY MONEY
MONEY MONEY MONEY MONEY

22. Realize Simplicity Is Not Poverty

John and Juan's situations show the true differences between simplicity and poverty. Both are thirty-two-year-old men, married with three kids, living in California's Sonoma County.

John is a contractor struggling to build up his remodeling business. Five days a week he drives his five-year-old Ford truck to the swanky side of the valley to work on $100,000 bathroom remodels for winery owners and telecom startup execs who drive new Range Rovers and Porsches. On Saturdays John walks away from his always-behind-schedule projects to attend a Tai Chi class and take his daughters ice skating. When he and his wife want to have a hot time on the town, they go swing dancing at the community center. They are saving a little money each month for retirement and college for the girls. Their three-bedroom ranch house is a little cramped, but John is gradually remodeling it into a small jewel. In a couple of years they hope to trade up to a two-acre parcel where John can build the passive-solar house he's been dreaming of.

Juan is from Sinaloa, Mexico, where his wife and three daughters remain. He sneaks over the border into the U.S. and hitchhikes up to Sonoma County every spring to work in construction, vineyards, and orchards. He lives about a mile from John, sharing a two-bedroom basement apartment with twelve other Mexican men, at least until the warmer summer weather arrives, when he usually moves out to sleep in an illegal campground by the river. Seven days a week he walks to the crossroads where day laborers wait, sometimes all day, to be picked up by men like John who need somebody for a few hours of building site cleanup, brush clearing, or digging irrigation ditches. Juan earns about $8 an hour, $5 of which he sends back to Mexico to support his mother, wife, and daughters. He misses them terribly and can't wait for December, when he sneaks back into Mexico for Christmas and a couple of months with his family.

John has embraced simplicity. Juan struggles to escape the clutches of poverty.

John has made a voluntary choice to drive a used truck, live within his means, stay out of debt, and so on. Juan's "choice" is more involuntary, dictated by desperate economic circumstances in Mexico.

John's simplicity is energizing, enabling him to enjoy life more; but Juan's poverty is exhausting and disabling. John could pass for twenty-five, whereas Juan looks forty.

John's simplicity is ennobling in a way. He can look in the mirror and feel proud of how he takes care of his family, himself, and his community, while living lightly and responsibly on the earth. Juan's poverty is degrading. When Americans in their Range Rovers and Porsches drive by him at the crossroads, they avert their eyes and he feels embarrassed and scared they will call the sheriff or the INS.

John's life is a dynamic balance between complexity and simplicity that can be emotionally and spiritually satisfying. Juan's life is a desperate balancing act that he often finds emotionally and spiritually painful.

John's simplicity is "aesthetic" as in "beautiful," based on the moderation of luxuries, careful choice of necessities, and an expectation of greater health and well-being. Juan's poverty is "ascetic" as in "austere," based on the impossibility of luxuries, self-deprivation of necessities, and the dire certainty that some day he will be too old, sick, or disabled to make the trip north any more. These distinctions mark the differences between a simple life that doesn't happen to contain much money, and an impoverished one. Even if you choose such a simple life, you are most emphatically not choosing "poverty."

23. Keep a Spending Diary

The late financial independence guru Joe Dominguez said, "Money is your life energy, don't throw it away." Since earning money requires you to give up some of your precious time alive on this planet, spending money carelessly is like giving up some of your life itself. Would you spend more carefully if every dollar you wasted took five minutes off your life expectancy?

You've probably heard this before—to get control of your money, you have to know what you're spending it on. You may have kept track of your expenses for a few weeks or tried to stick to a monthly budget. These budgeting efforts seldom have lasting results beyond making you feel like a spendthrift.

Keeping a spending diary in service of life simplification isn't really a budgeting function at all. It's more like free therapy, or a spiritual discipline whose purpose is gaining control of your life energy. The spending diary raises your awareness of your unconscious motivations and allows you to meet your emotional needs in ways that are more direct, appropriate, and affordable than throwing cash at them.

For example, Sally was the mother of two teenage boys, assistant manager of a drugstore, wife of a computer engineer, and avid tennis player. She and her husband Bill earned good salaries, but they were in debt and worried about paying for their sons' college educations and their own eventual retirement. Sally wrote down every cent she spent, every day for three months. At the end of each month she tabulated her expenditures under categories such as food, shelter, transportation, entertainment, and so on.

Sally found that she was spending three times what she previously estimated on clothes, eating out, and weekend vacations. She realized that shopping for and buying new clothes after work relaxed her, eating out was an escape from the chaos of dinnertime at home, and weekend getaways were a very expensive way of spending time alone with her husband. She further realized that she could relax by taking long walks or playing tennis. She could calm dinnertime by forbidding loud music and teen visitors on school nights. She could spend time with Bill on the walks or just lock the bedroom door and tell the boys to leave them alone.

You can keep your own spending diary in any form that's convenient; just carry pen and paper with you. Whether it's twenty cents for gum or $2,000 for the mortgage payment, write it down to the penny, as close as possible to the instant you spend it. Don't round off or estimate or wait till the end of the day. Being obsessively timely and accurate is the spiritual part of the discipline. It keeps you exquisitely conscious of the act of spending money, countering the common tendency to blank out, detach, repress, or otherwise become unconscious of what you're doing.

At the end of each month, put each expense into categories that make sense to you and add them up. Here are some suggested column headings: food, shelter, entertainment, transportation, education, health, recreation, utilities, charity. Combine or expand these categories to fit your lifestyle and spending patterns. Under most headings you will probably want subcategories. For instance, food can be subdivided into groceries, lunch at work, dinners out, and snacks. Or you might put dinners out in the entertainment or recreation categories.

Remember that the goal is consciousness, not making a budget or making yourself feel bad. Then, like Sally did, examine your spending patterns for what they tell you about your needs and values. You can then find less expensive and more fulfilling ways to meet those needs and live your values.

24. Take a Spending Break

Take a good look at your spending diary (#23). Are you surprised by how much you spent overall? If so, rest assured that this is typical—most of us spend more than we realize, simply out of habit.

For example, were you shocked to find you ate more than half your meals away from home? Even a daily stop for coffee and a pastry can add up to well over a hundred dollars a month, and regular lunches and dinners out make a much bigger dent in your bank account. There are also all those seemingly small expenditures: clothing you bought simply because it was on sale; shoes you picked up to lift your mood after a bad day at work; the armload of magazines you don't have time to read; an "extra" set of something you already have at home, just in case you might need it someday. When you spend money without really thinking about it, it's all too easy to:

- rack up debts

- lose track of the value money holds for you

- clutter up your life with possessions and financial insecurity at the same time

- confuse your wants with your needs

- use purchases as an emotional crutch

Because we're bombarded with "buy" messages that set out to skew our perspective, it's not surprising that we have these tendencies. For some of us, spending gets out of control. But even if yours isn't out of control—if you can afford what you buy—it's still instructive to try a spending moratorium. You may even find that some of the meaningful things you thought you *couldn't* afford (such as getting out of debt, saving for the future, traveling, working fewer hours, planning an early retirement) are actually well within your reach.

The length of your moratorium is an individual choice. Thirty days is a good goal, because it's at that point that you'll start to see how excessive purchasing adds up over time. However, if that's too daunting, try two weeks instead. During the moratorium, buy only groceries and essential personal items. You may wish to rethink your concept of "essential"—just keep your personal simplifying goals in mind, and check your spending diary for a reminder of those areas where you feel you're spending too much. Every time you decide to make do rather than buy, or resist a shopping impulse that you would otherwise have succumbed to, record the amount saved. At the end of the designated time, this list will tell you a lot about your spending impulses.

You can even turn the "making do" aspect of the moratorium into a game of sorts, finding items you already own that can stand in for things you're tempted to purchase. (And in the process, you'll probably start to sort out the clutter in your storage spaces—see #5, Get Organized, for more on decluttering and organizing.) In addition to shopping in your own home, you may find that borrowing and trading come in handy here (see #31, Swap and Share, for some tips). At the end, you'll have saved a good deal of cash, and you may decide you're just clever enough to keep this moratorium thing going for another month. Or two.

25. Shop Smart and Simple

In the course of simplifying your life, you'll reduce your consumption of many of the goods that you once thought were indispensable. But of course you'll still need to buy things. The trick is to buy the *right* things—things that please you, things that last, things you feel good about owning.

Spencer and Jane had a shopping problem—they'd be the first to admit it. Their problem wasn't that they shopped too much; they just didn't shop very carefully. Take the living-room curtains. They'd vaguely wanted a new set for a couple of years, but weren't truly motivated to find just the right pair. When they finally happened upon some that they liked—and on sale too!—they snapped them right up. But after the curtains were hung, it became clear that they weren't quite long enough, and that they kind of clashed with the couch. So it was back to the same choice they had made many times before: hassle with the store about returning a sale item, or look at those stupid curtains every day and feel like clods for choosing the wrong thing *again*.

Clothing was even worse. Jane tended to shop the sales, because it seemed crazy to pay top dollar. Then, since she'd shoved her way through the crowds, it felt like a waste to go home empty-handed. And that sparkly blue dress was only thirty dollars! It was true that she didn't really have a place to wear it—at least not this season—but it might come in handy someday. Because she didn't like her wardrobe, she was always tempted to hit the stores for another try. Spencer also had a problem with clothes shopping. Since his office had moved to a "business casual" dress code, he had to buy new things to bridge his old standby business suits and his very slouchy preferences for weekend wear. But it seemed a shame to spend loads of money on simple khakis and button-downs when he had all those nice suits. So he hit the local discount emporium with Jane, and ended up with a whole pile of shirts and pants that seemed okay. The problem was that after just a couple of washings, they were decidedly less spiffy than business casual required. And once he'd taken a closer look at the labels, the idea that the clothes were probably made in sweatshops started to bother him as well. So it's three strikes for Spencer and Jane.

What about you? With the right mindset, you can avoid making similar mistakes. Of course, when you're working on simplifying, it becomes even more important to choose wisely. Ideally, you're spending less money, time, and effort on your belongings. Making the wrong call on a purchase can throw a wrench in the works. Here are ways to avoid those mistakes:

- Don't just wander the aisles (or the Internet). From cars to cookware, it helps to know what you need or want beforehand. You'll be less likely to make an unwise impulse buy.

- Before you even start, be sure you don't already own something that can serve the same purpose.

- When you know exactly what you plan to purchase, consider buying online to save gasoline and time. If you don't want to do that, at least call ahead to make sure the store has your item in stock.

- Examine the quality of each potential purchase carefully. Will it last? Remember, quality goods are less expensive in the long run, and you'll save yourself the trouble of shopping for replacement items later.

- Buy the one thing you really love instead of ten things you kind of like. You'll feel satiated and be less likely to spend compulsively.

- Is the item aesthetically pleasing and well designed? Can you see yourself enjoying it for a good long time?

- Is it nonpolluting? Is there a locally produced option? Do the manufacturer's ethics jibe with yours? Do you feel good sending your hard-earned money out into the world in exchange for this item?

After you've made your choices, resolve to take good care of your new possessions, and repair and recycle them whenever possible.

26. Find a Better Hobby

Let's say you meet someone new who asks you what you like to do in your spare time. You love to talk about your hobbies: tennis, gardening, woodworking, Thai cooking, shopping. Wait, shopping? Would you actually put it on your list of hobbies? If you're a typical American, you spend as much or more time shopping as on activities you would classify as hobbies. And much of this time is probably spent on so-called "recreational" shopping—shopping for "fun" as opposed to buying groceries and basic necessities. But how much fun are you having when you hit the mall? How much satisfaction do you get from your purchases?

Here are a few of the pitfalls that may result from using shopping as a hobby:

- It keeps your energy on the surface level of acquiring possessions rather than freeing it for deeper pursuits.

- It encourages excessive focus on perfection in personal appearance and home décor.

- It covers up (or even worsens) issues of low self-esteem, boredom, and loneliness.

- It threatens financial well-being and security.

Of course, most people don't shop so much that they risk bankruptcy or serious emotional problems. But many of us spend enough money and time on this socially acceptable pastime to prevent us from achieving some of our goals and desires. Emily's story is a good example.

At age thirty-three, Emily was deeply frustrated that she and her husband were still a few years away from their dream of home ownership, and even more upset that she didn't know where their money was going. After all, she and Robert made above-average salaries, had been in the work world for ten years, and didn't go in for major luxury goods like expensive cars. They were stay-at-home types who preferred to relax around the house at the end of the workday. After two months of keeping a spending diary (see # 23), it became very clear where the money went—and it was a little bit scary. Emily was inspired to sort through the previous several years' worth of receipts to get a better idea of how they were spending over time.

Their average annual expenditures on personal goods looked something like this:

Emily's work clothing: $1,800/year

Robert's work clothing: $1,500/year

Combined casual clothing: $1,500/year

Furniture: $1,980/year

Other home décor: $1,680/year

Home electronics: $2,000/year

Total: $10,460/year

Of course, not all of the expenses were totally discretionary. Emily and Robert had to look presentable for work, but they knew they could reduce these costs substantially—neither had a lot of their work ego riding on their wardrobe. Casual clothing could be cut back too, since like most of us they gravitated to the same comfortable pair of jeans on weekends anyway. The home décor and electronics total came as the biggest shock. In their urge to create a nest, over the course of their marriage they had spent the equivalent of a couple of house down payments, filling up a succession of rented apartments when what they really wanted was a place to call their own. Inspired by a goal that suddenly seemed attainable, they found it much easier to replace trips to the mall with the other hobbies on their lists.

27. Embrace the Spirit of Giving

As you take steps to simplify, your attitude about gift-giving (and receiving) may change. Kim and Chris were a young couple who had started simplifying their lives as a New Year's resolution. They scaled back their work hours in order to spend more time at home with their young son Bryson, and they reduced their expenditures substantially in order to get by on less income. As the year passed they realized they really enjoyed this new focus on family time. But when the first holiday season of their newly simplified life rolled around, they were naturally apprehensive about that part of the season that has become the focus in our culture: gifts.

Checking their budgets from the previous three years, they found that they had spent a couple thousand dollars a year on gifts for more than twenty family members, plus friends and work associates—all for presents that had seemed pretty modest at the time. So where did all that money go? The sheer number of people they cared about and wanted to give to meant that the total added up fast. The big question was whether anyone would even notice if they didn't spend it.

But their concern with the gifts wasn't just about the money; they also wanted to share the benefits of the simpler life with their loved ones, and they had a feeling that another sweater or pair of pajamas wasn't really going to help. And of course they wanted to avoid the crush of shoppers at the mall. To start, they made up a list of all the people they normally gave to, as well as a list of alternative gifts, including edible items, services, and charitable donations. As they planned their gift list, they tried to carefully match recipients with gifts they would likely enjoy and appreciate. That meant that their parents, who had no need or desire for more possessions, received charitable donations in their names to a hunger relief organization and specially commissioned holiday collages by Bryson. Their siblings who lived locally—and who were enormously overworked—received certificates (again crafted by Bryson) inviting them to drop off their kids for several "cousins' weekends" at Kim and Chris' place. (They secretly hoped their siblings might use this time to work on simplifying their lives, but a gift is best with no strings attached!)

Instead of the usual battery-operated trendy toys, all the kids in the family got art supply kits: tackle boxes from the five-and-dime filled with art supplies as well as fabric scraps, ribbons, and found objects like buttons, shells, and stones. To friends who liked to cook, they gave homemade flavored vinegars (very easy to create) or store-bought gourmet jams and sauces. For their many friends without the epicurean instinct, they stuck to good old-fashioned cookies and candies they made themselves. Though they were a bit nervous about this new way of giving, they had no need to be, because they were overwhelmed with thanks for their thoughtful, personal presents.

They changed their ways of receiving gifts as well. When asked what they wanted, they requested practical items to replace things that had worn out; when there was nothing they needed, they asked friends and family to give them time instead. Some of the responses they got were babysitting offers, invitations to the movies, a new decorative paint job for their bathroom, and a whole week of early-morning dog walking so everyone could sleep in while Bryson was on school vacation.

How might changing your perception of gifts—both giving and receiving them—change your life?

28. Break the Money Habit

It starts so innocently. You've barely learned how to walk and talk, you're still too short to see the top of the candy counter, and Mommy gives you a nickel to buy your own gummy worm. Later you get chores and an allowance, your first job and a paycheck, your first bills and a bank account. You want to do what others do and have what others have, so you buy your first car, your first suit, your first big vacation, your first house. It's a simple, natural, inevitable progression. Most of the time it feels like growing up to be a big person, a solid citizen, a productive member of society.

But sometimes it feels like a downward spiral into dysfunction and dependence. You want a better car, so you save up and buy one that is a little more than you can really afford. It's too nice to leave on the street, so you rent a garage. The garage is a long walk from the apartment, so you start thinking about buying a house. Your favorite pusher—the same Mommy who gave you your first nickel—lends you a down payment. Suddenly your wistful urge for a more reliable car has metastasized into a $100,000 mortgage and a long commute to that nonprofit gig that matches your values but doesn't pay much. You take a job with a cereal company that also owns nuclear power plants—distasteful, but they're paying the serious bucks you need to make your nut every month.

Is it possible that you are addicted to money? Check out what happens when you take a commonly used substance abuse questionnaire and replace the references to alcohol and drugs with references to money and spending:

- Has anybody ever told you that you spend too much money?

- Do you sometimes think that money is causing problems in your life?

- Do you sometimes spend more money than you intended to?

- Does your spending sometimes feel out of control?

- Have money problems hurt your relationships, job, life, or freedom?

- Do you have to spend more money than you used to, to get the same enjoyment?

- When you have no money to spend, do you feel sick, depressed, anxious, or angry?

Most of us would have to answer yes to all of these questions. Money routinely destroys relationships, impairs judgment, warps behavior, limits freedom, harms health, corrupts morals, fosters dependence, and causes painful emotions. It has all the hallmarks of a classic addictive substance like cocaine or heroin.

Substance abuse is widely considered a genetically based disorder that should be treated like a disease. There are research programs, detox centers, and twelve-step meetings every day of the week. But money addiction is still not recognized as an official disease or an important problem by most people. Beyond a few compulsive spending support groups and get-out-of-debt gurus, help for money addiction is not readily available. You are on your own.

Unfortunately, you can't go cold turkey and swear off money the way you can abstain from scotch or amphetamines. Money addiction is more like an eating disorder in the sense that you can't stop spending in today's world any more than you can stop eating. As with eating disorders, moderation is the key to controlling money addiction.

By simplifying your life, you will reduce your addictive money behavior. You will find your own comfortable place along the continuum from brown rice subsistence to the full-tilt Beverly Hills Boogie.

29. Practice Self-Reliance

In #10, Hire it Out, we advised you to delegate those tasks you just can't manage yourself. On the other hand, sometimes people today get overspecialized. Sandy, for example, was a "Branch/Net/Sys/Admin" for a big bank. She spent sixty hours a week keeping a complex computer network up and running, so that others could do the actual work of banking. She then used her impressive salary to have everything else in her life done for her: restaurants cooked her meals, housekeepers cleaned her house, mechanics fixed her car, gardeners mowed her lawn, accountants did her taxes, and a gift buying service even bought Christmas and birthday presents for her mom and her boyfriend Brian.

One Christmas Sandy's personal local area network crashed. Through a fluke of crossed signals, her gift service sent mom a jumbo bottle of Seraphina's All-Night Edible Love-Making Oil and Brian received a quilted satin housecoat and a subscription to *Our Methodist Messenger*. Sandy took it as a sign that she had to stop paying others to live her life for her.

Naturally the first task she reclaimed from the service industry was buying gifts. Then she started cooking breakfast for herself and Brian on Sunday mornings instead of going out. She kept her gardener, but reserved one window box for her own pale-green thumb. Even these small steps toward self-reliance made her feel more like a three-dimensional person instead of a walking, talking computer manual.

What could you do for yourself that you now have done for you? Some ideas:

- Change your own oil.
- Cook new gourmet recipes.
- Give haircuts to family members.
- Fix a bike.
- Mow the lawn.
- Paint the bathroom.

- Tile the floor.
- Do your own taxes.
- Build some bookshelves.
- Design a Web site.
- Bake bread.
- Reupholster your favorite chair.

What else? What costs you a lot to have done, while making you feel ignorant or incompetent? Ignore the voice inside that says, "Yeah, but I don't know how ... I could never learn." The world is full of classes and self-help books. A call to the community college and a stroll through the Yellow Pages or the Internet will quiet most "Yeah, buts."

Learning to do something new for yourself has many payoffs. You can save money and raise your standard of living without working more hours a week. You can have more cash to spend on things you really can't provide for yourself, like dentistry, jet travel, or world-class opera.

As you do more for yourself at home, you start tuning into the process rather than the product. The feel of the soil becomes more important than the tomatoes and zucchini. Bringing order to chaos becomes more important than cleaning the bathroom. Perhaps the greatest benefit of learning to do things for yourself is your growing sense of pride in your accomplishments, which raises your self-esteem and your confidence that you can take care of yourself. You become more resilient, more stress-proof, and more able to cope with emergencies.

And besides, it's just plain fun to learn new things. Some people have so much fun they get carried away with self-reliance. They try to bake all their own bread, feel guilty when they buy store bread, and secretly wish they could grow their own wheat, culture their own yeast, and mine their own salt. Seek balance and simplicity as you seek self-reliance, and above all, have fun.

30. Invest Wisely in Your Future

More Americans are investing in the stock market than ever before, and at younger and younger ages. You may be one of them. If you do it right, investing in stocks can be a great way to diversify your portfolio (beyond home ownership, for example, which makes up the largest proportion of most households' wealth). It also allows you to take advantage of the successes of companies other than the one you work for. Done wrong, however, stock market investing can result in the loss of time, money, or both.

But should you buy individual stocks or invest in a mutual fund? That depends on how much time you have to devote to this pursuit. Think about it this way: there are people out there who study the markets full time, and even they can't always pick the winners. So you may lose money and time trying to keep up. A recent study by UC Davis economists Brad Barber and Terrance Odean found that the households that traded stocks most frequently performed substantially worse than other households, an effect the researchers attribute to overconfidence. The perils of overconfidence aside, trading frequently also means you'll rack up transaction fees. When you take a look at how this approach eats into your earnings, the returns of a well-chosen, low-fee mutual fund tend to pull ahead.

The skyrocketing stock market of recent years had many investors thinking they couldn't lose. Many new investors jumped in with both feet and purchased individual stocks, often based on no particular knowledge of an industry, just the same newspaper articles everyone else was reading. As could be expected, many folks lost their shirts when prices started to drop, especially those investors engaged in risky behavior like buying on margin.

Online trading has changed things as well. If you know what you're doing, it can be simpler; however, in many cases it leads people to buy and sell much more often than they otherwise would, turning investing into an obsessive hobby or what amounts to a second job. We've heard of more than one person trading online who, prompted by a simple point-and-click button, jumped into buying on margin without realizing he could turn his big balance into a big debt overnight. Barber and Odean have studied the online investment phenomenon as well, and found that investors who switch to online trading fit a certain profile—they had typically been beating the market substantially before they switched. After switching, however, they traded more frequently and less profitably—performing worse than the market instead of better.

Here are a few tips to keep in mind:

- Market cycles are long, so be prepared to ride out the lows.

- Don't move your investments around excessively. Put your money somewhere and leave it there. The money you save in transaction costs alone will add substantially to your overall gain.

- For long-term investment strategies, consider a mutual fund that tracks the S&P 500 or another broad-based market index. You won't need to keep track of how the fund manager is doing, and history indicates that you're likely to beat the majority of funds and individual stocks over time. Another bonus: you'll typically pay lower fees.

- Choose a financial services provider that can handle all your needs. That way you won't have to divide your energies dealing with a number of different companies.

- Remember that financial planners are in effect salespeople—they earn money by selling you a product. Don't assume that they are acting in your best interest.

- Make the maximum contribution to vehicles that give you favorable tax treatment, such as IRAs and 401(k)s, before investing in other opportunities.

- To keep it simple and to keep yourself on track in building your portfolio, add to your investments at regularly scheduled times. Don't worry about the price at which you're buying.

31. Swap and Share

Bartering—trading goods and/or services rather than exchanging money for them—may not seem like the most feasible way to simplify your life. First you have the "double coincidence" factor: you must have what the other person wants, and vice-versa. You might have to spend some time and effort (and a bit of moxie) to find a match. Plus, if you're trading a service rather than an object, you need to spend time providing that service. So, yes, barter does have its inefficiencies—that's why we also have money! However, bartering has its benefits too: you save money, and you get the satisfaction of providing something that someone else values, whether it's a service or a good.

Although you may not personally know anyone who's doing it, bartering is on the rise among individuals and between businesses. Plenty of bartering is very informal in nature and happens serendipitously. Jeff, a public-interest attorney who works for a meager salary, was asked by an acquaintance to vet a contract for a real-estate deal. In exchange, Jeff received a free stay at a mountain getaway that would otherwise have been out of his price range. But rather than waiting for something to happen, you may want to be a little more proactive. Ask around your neighborhood or your office to see if any opportunities are going unnoticed. Mike, who runs a bakery, got in the habit of keeping bags of cookies in his truck. Any time he was in the market for something, he asked whether a barter deal might suit the other party. And often it did: he got free photo developing, bags of fresh vegetables from the farmers' market, and parts for his bike.

But you don't even have to rely on happenstance these days, because there are a number of bartering clubs on the scene. While these clubs, newsletters, and Web sites differ in levels of formality, they share one goal: helping individuals or businesses connect so they can exchange goods and services. Some help you find the person who both wants what you have and has what you want. Others remove the double coincidence problem: when you provide a service or good, you receive a form of currency that allows you to "purchase" anything on the network. Some bartering clubs and networks can be found on the Internet, while plenty of others operate through word of mouth or via newsletters. Some are free of charge, while others charge a fee for membership or for each transaction. Through a newsletter, Monique offered private yoga instruction in exchange for the new kitchen table she wanted. Clark, a small-business owner, used an online network to offer his marketing skills in exchange for database management assistance.

Sharing ownership of stuff you don't use every day can work well too. You save money, and you don't have to store as much. You might feel sheepish at first, so start slowly. Ask family members or close friends to enter into a sharing arrangement, then branch out to acquaintances and neighbors if it works for you. That's how Roger got started. A sports fiend, he was trying to break his habit of rushing out to buy the newest gear for each pursuit that caught his fancy. He asked one friend to split the cost of a pair of snowshoes, and he asked if he could borrow the sea kayak his brother didn't have time to use, in exchange for the use of Roger's bike. He eventually entered into a tool-sharing relationship with his next-door neighbor.

While it may take a bit of effort to get started, bartering and sharing may soon become second nature to you. After all, remember second grade and the deals you used to make with baseball cards and marbles?

relationships

RELATIONSHIPS RELATIONSHIPS
RELATIONSHIPS RELATIONSHIPS RELATIONSHIPS RELATIONSHIPS
RELATIONSHIPS RELATIONSHIPS RELATIONSHIPS RELATIONSHIPS
RELATIONSHIPS RELATIONSHIPS RELATIONSHIPS ✧

32. Survey Your Tribe

Humans evolved in tribal situations where they seldom interacted with more than fifty people in a lifetime. The social environment has changed in the last thousand years, but that is an evolutionary blink of the eye. Today you have exactly the same body and nervous system and social instincts as your tribal ancestors. But thanks to urban density, electronic communication, and global consumer culture, you'll meet thousands of people in your lifetime, and be expected to remain "acquainted" with three or four hundred of them.

No wonder you can't remember people's names! Your brain is not designed to keep track of that many individuals. And why should you have to? You don't really need to maintain tenuous connections to people with whom you have nothing in common. Businesspeople make a big deal out of "networking," never letting a casual acquaintance go unexploited. Don't fall for that sales manager's pep talk. Nets are for catching fish, not building real community.

Focus your love and energy on the dozen or so people closest to you—your immediate family, dearest friends, sanest relatives, and nicest neighbors. Say no to the rest so that you can reduce the number of people you visit, call, entertain, and just "keep in touch with." Cut truly toxic people out of your life entirely. They are a major and unacceptable complication.

Here is an exercise. Get out your address book, Christmas card list, e-mail list, membership lists, alumni lists, phone trees, and so on. Go through each list and mark people who meet most of these criteria:

You have talked to them in the last year.

You like or love them.

You respect their opinions.

You trust their judgment.

You value their approval.

You'd loan them money.

You'd loan them your car.

You want to keep them in your life.

You'd really miss them if they died or moved away.

These people are in your tribe. How big is it? There may be a handful or as many as fifty. These are the family members and friends who make up the essential social fabric of your life. These are the keepers, the ones you want to invite over for dinner, go on vacation with, share apartments with, go into businesses with, appoint as guardians for your children, make executors of your will, and so on.

The rest are the losers, in the sense that you could lose them from your life without missing them much. Some are like grumpy Uncle Max or your scatterbrained niece whom you can't entirely avoid. Others are clients, customers, bosses, neighbors, friends of friends, or club members with whom you must sometimes interact. But you don't owe them any serious time, attention, or entrée into your life.

Many on your lists are nearly forgotten school chums, distant cousins, ex-neighbors, friends of relatives, and relatives of friends who don't even rate a Christmas card. Take them off the lists and forget them.

Occasionally someone you don't like or want in your life will want you to come to dinner or sit on a committee whose work you don't care passionately for. Tell such people you are too stressed out, trying to simplify your life, and unable to participate. Don't worry that saying no will seem "not nice," or that you will miss out on meeting potential new members of your tribe. If they are really potential members of your tribe, they will understand and come round again. If they are not potential members of your tribe, their opinions of your niceness don't count and they will fade away.

33. Mix It Up

If your calendar is filled with coffee with one friend, lunch with another, and dinner with yet another, consider consolidating them into one event. You can enjoy everyone's company at once—and perhaps enable different friends of yours to become friends with each other. You may spend a few more minutes arranging such a gathering, but you'll save lots of time overall.

Maria started her Wednesday Night Dinner tradition with a group of five disparate friends about five years ago. It's now an institution on the first Wednesday of every month, and the original invitees, formerly casual acquaintances, now know each other well and look forward to getting together at Maria's house. The day and location don't shift around, so it's easy to keep track of when and where they're supposed to show up. Maria always cooks the main course, Jeff always brings a salad, Sally and Jessica bring drinks, Chris brings bread, and Sam brings dessert. (The routine assignments eliminate the need for advance planning among the participants.)

You can also invite a bunch of friends to join a reading group—you'll have incentive to make time for that hot new novel, and you'll also have built-in time to catch up with your pals. Just make an effort to gather together friends who have at least vaguely similar literary tastes. You can take turns choosing the book and hosting the event. Sticking to the same day of the week (the third Thursday of the month, for example) helps everyone with the planning. The host can provide snacks—nothing too complicated is necessary.

At holiday times especially, it can be hard to stay caught up with all your pals in addition to coping with the demands of the season. How about inviting friends over to make holiday decorations? Choose a few items to make—Thanksgiving centerpieces, Christmas tree decorations—and ask each person to bring one of the items necessary for the project. You'll get to see friends during this busy time, and you'll get some fun, inexpensive projects done. (See #27, Embrace the Spirit of Giving, for an example of keeping the holidays simple and social.) This also works great for holiday baking; a few extra pairs of hands make a big difference in getting goodies baked and decorated. At times other than the holidays, the same kind of get-together can also be fun: make a batch of birthday cards, valentines, or all-occasion cards using rubber stamps, glitter pens, photographs, buttons, ribbons, paper collage—you name it.

A coffeehouse club is another good way to stay in touch with a minimum of planning. Just choose a favorite spot where people can drop by on Sunday morning or a weekday evening. Or a tasting gathering at your home can bring together various people from your life. It doesn't matter what you taste: wine, cheeses, exotic fruits. The structure of the event gives guests a low-pressure way to interact. (Also check out #38, Make Over Your Social Life, for ways to make your social life less expensive and more satisfying.)

34. Let Go of the Past

How much time do you spend reliving and regretting the past? Do you rehearse your list of grievances against parents, siblings, or ex-partners? Mourn missed opportunities? Pine for long-lost children, family, or friends? Dwell on old pains, fears, mistakes, or failures?

Hanging on to the past complicates your life by stealing the time and energy you need to cope with life today, in the here and now. You can simplify your life by acknowledging and learning from your past without letting it dominate and define you.

Try this simple exercise. Draw three columns on a sheet of paper. At the top of the first column, write "My worst bad memory." In the second column, write "What it taught me," and in the third column, write "How I can let go of it now."

For the first column, ask yourself: "Who hurt me? Whom did I hurt? Who died or left me? What did I lose? What opportunity did I miss? What mistake did I make? What did I lose?" Write down the answer or answers. In the second column, write the positive lesson you learned, even if you have to make up a positive spin on the experience. In the third column, "reframe" the memory with a phrase that puts it into perspective. Look for something short and memorable that you can say to yourself whenever you recall the bad memory, something that will help you cut the regret session short and get on with your life. This letting-go phrase can be a cliché or truism such as "water under the bridge," or just a single word like "serenity"—as long as it has meaning to you.

Ben and Laurie were divorced after being unhappily married for six years. Here's how Ben did this exercise:

1. Laurie left me.

2. I learned not to make commitments lightly, and that relationships need constant maintenance.

3. I let go of the past by telling myself I have survived, and what doesn't kill me makes me stronger.

Here's how Laurie did it:

1. I left Ben.

2. I learned not to define myself in terms of other people.

3. I let go of the past by reminding myself that I'm older and wiser now and that I can act as the adult I am now, not the insecure kid I was back then.

Marta's teenage daughter died in a head-on collision four years ago, and she still thinks about her almost every day. Here is Marta's exercise:

1. Julie died in a car accident.

2. I learned that life is precious and precarious, and that it must be treasured.

3. I let go by thinking she wouldn't want me to be sad, and by doing something for my other daughter.

John spent the first twenty-nine years of his life trying to please his critical, moralizing parents. Here is how he started working on letting go:

1. My parents constantly criticized and belittled me.

2. I learned you can't judge yourself by others' standards.

3. I let go by forgiving them as fallible, limited people; I remember that I am a valuable, competent person; I keep my distance and stifle all impulses to seek their approval now.

It's also important to realize that there *is* such a thing as post-traumatic stress disorder, in which you startle easily, have vivid flashbacks to past traumas, have difficulty relating to others, and suffer extreme emotional reactions of anxiety, anger, or depression. If you have serious trauma in your past such as abuse, an accident, violence, or a natural disaster, you will need therapeutic help to come to terms with it.

35. Give Your Kids the Gift of Time

When you look back on your childhood, what do you wish you could recapture? Chances are you dream fondly of chasing the ice-cream truck and running through the sprinklers, teasing the dog and hanging out with friends. Now think for a minute about what your own kids will remember about their youth. Do they have time to just be kids? It's not such a crazy question, because it's increasingly common for young children to lead highly regimented lives. For many, especially those whose parents have the most to give them financially, life is all about achieving the very best in school, sports, the arts—sometimes all at the same time. It's enough to make even most adults wish for a cookie and a very long nap.

Stop and think about it: do your children have schedules as overstuffed as a hard-charging corporate vice-president's? If they're overwhelmed with activities, they may end up suffering from some of the same problems that led you to seek a simpler existence: anxiety, a feeling of being overwhelmed, and fatigue.

Because their son Jasper had always loved listening to music, Jack and Tammy got him started on the piano at a young age. He showed an aptitude for it, and never complained about having to practice every day. When he turned eight, they added violin lessons, with the best teacher around, who happened to live thirty miles away. The extra driving didn't bother them, because naturally they wanted the best for their son. When Jasper complained of being picked last for school teams, it seemed natural to get him involved in sports to bring his confidence level up. Since he took to music so quickly, they assumed he'd enjoy learning a new skill. So they sat down as a family and decided on soccer in the fall and baseball in the spring. Jack and Tammy quickly became the most ardent fans on the sidelines.

But soon Jasper was having a hard time waking up in the morning, and his formerly stellar grades slipped a bit. At first his parents thought a tutor might help him bring his marks back up, but then they realized he was just plain worn out. It was clear that something had to give, and they decided it ought to be Jasper's choice. He decided to keep piano lessons year-round, soccer in the fall, and a multisport camp for a few weeks in the summer—and happily gave up the rest.

Elena is a good example of what can happen when a child's schedule gets out of control and then stays that way. She had been involved in lots of activities from the time she was ten, but by her sophomore year in high school, she had club meetings almost every day before class started, a full schedule of college prep courses, and activities every day after school. In the evenings there was a serious amount of homework to be done. Elena was so caught up in being a well-rounded success story—the kind of student that every college wants—that having time to just be herself didn't seem like a feasible option. And wasn't college a good excuse for sticking to a breakneck pace? This *was* her future on the line. She fretted constantly about her prospects, and worried that no matter how much she did, it wouldn't be enough. After talking to the school counselor, her parents explained to Elena that doing too much was almost as bad as not doing enough. Spreading herself so thin caused several problems. She wasn't enjoying life, she wasn't doing her best at any one thing, and she stood a pretty good chance of ruining her health and her state of mind in the process. It took a bit of convincing, but her parents coaxed her to give up enough activities so that she had two free afternoons a week, plus one weekend day. Her anxiety eased up, and she had more fun with the remaining activities.

So, since you're working on changes, why not help your kids discover the joys of the simple life? Simplicity is not just about activities, but about your whole approach to life: work, money, everything you value and cherish. Having these discussions now will benefit you and your children for years to come.

36. Think for Yourself

One of the major complicating factors in our lives is that we so often do things a certain way just because that's "how it's done." You may find thoughts like these cropping up in your conversation or just in your mind: That's how everyone does it. That's the way my mom did it. That's what I'm supposed to do. Well, I just *have* to—what will people think?

Melissa was forced to confront her people-pleasing tendencies during the year of her engagement. Her initial preference was to have a very small wedding, with just family and a few friends. But when she started on the guest list, she realized that during her long relationship with her partner, they had developed more close friendships than would fit into a tiny wedding, not to mention all the extended family members they wanted to invite. So the tiny wedding grew, but that felt right. They could throw a bigger, casual wedding, maybe with a potluck reception, in their backyard. No problem.

Melissa then asked for advice from friends who had had home weddings, and found out that Pete's family had called in a landscaper and Melanie's mom had had her house repainted. And what about a tent in case it rains? And where will you put all the tables, because people can't eat standing up, can they? Don't forget, the out-of-towners might find our summer weather a bit chilly, so you'll probably want some of those big gas heaters. You have to have a professional photographer or you'll regret it. Don't be silly, of course you need caterers, but are you sure your kitchen is really big enough for them to work in?

Not surprisingly, doubt crept in and threatened to stay, especially as Melissa did more research and found that it was easy to spend the price of a car (a really *nice* car) on a six-hour event. The wedding was supposed to be a celebration of this new phase of their lives, but it was starting to feel like a big hassle and an obligation to someone else's ideals.

So Melissa looked at the list again, this time more carefully. All the people on that list were invited because she and her fiancé wanted to share their big day with them. So cutting back the list felt like the wrong solution. Then she hit on something:

these weren't people she and her partner were trying to impress or trick into thinking they were something other than what they were. So why should she repaint the house or put in a new lawn, or pay a small fortune for catering? Her married friends had made their decisions about what they wanted, and they went out and got it. That didn't mean Melissa had to want the same thing. And yes, she ended up with exactly the wedding she wanted, on terms that felt right to her.

If you have a problem thinking for yourself, it would be wise to keep a diary to help you sort out your people-pleasing habits and beliefs. Next time you catch yourself doing something that you're only doing for someone else—reluctantly going to dinner with people you don't really like, overspending on a gift for a casual friend because she always spends a lot on you, going into debt for some event or possession simply because it's the norm to do it—write it down. In one column, list the reasons you feel you "must" do something. Include the negative feelings that will come up if you don't do it, such as guilt. In another column, list the negative feelings that come up when you go ahead and *do* do that something, such as feeling like a doormat, being bored when you hang out with people you don't like, or getting angry at yourself when you spend money you don't have. Finally, imagine how you would feel if you made decisions based on your own needs and desires.

It may take an adjustment of habit to truly think for yourself, but the extra bit of effort is a big step toward living your ideal simple life.

37. Draw the Line

Is it possible to simplify your life by saying "no" more often? If you don't have well-defined boundaries, the answer may be "yes." (There *are* people whose boundaries are too strict—who say no perhaps too often, who won't explore new ideas—but we'll venture a guess that they don't go on overload trying to please everyone, a propensity that may have led you to this book in the first place.)

So, what *are* boundaries, anyway? They're simply limits. When you choose who and what you want in your life, you're exercising your boundaries. If your boundaries are insufficient, your life will be full of things and relationships that aren't fulfilling or even safe, and that you don't want. Our boundaries come from our deeply held beliefs about who we are, what we're capable of, and what we deserve in life, and they encompass everything we know—or think we know—about ourselves. So boundaries involve our relationships with others and with ourselves.

We can't survive without boundaries. And we can't live a fulfilled and happy life without the *right* boundaries. Early in life, your boundaries were formed around how your parents and other caregivers reacted to you. As time went on, you tested those boundaries and adjusted them over and over again based on new experiences and changes in your beliefs. Throughout this process, the reactions of others continued to influence how you saw yourself.

If your boundaries are weak, the key to strengthening them is to learn to value yourself. You must care enough to protect yourself and your interests, which means saying no sometimes. As you try to simplify, the areas of your life that are affected by weak boundaries are most likely pretty obvious to you. You bend to pressure from a friend who wants to go out on a weeknight, then oversleep and miss your train in the morning. You don't speak up when you're overloaded at work—instead you stay late every night for a month to handle the extra project your boss gave you.

There are so many possibilities for weak boundaries to complicate your life: that committee you "have to" serve on because the other members say you're the best planner; hours every week on the phone with your brother, rehashing the same problems he told you about *last* week. But there are ways to defend your boundaries. Here are a few things to try:

- Promise yourself that at a certain signal, you will stop and redirect the situation to protect yourself: "When I realize I'm starting to give in to pressure, I'll stop the conversation for a moment and figure out what *I* want."

- Be specific when making business and personal commitments. If you're honest about your intended level of involvement, there's less chance of a misunderstanding. And if one does occur, you'll feel better about asserting your needs if you were clear about them in the first place.

- Know who you are, how you function best, and what you want. Keep your self-knowledge and your goals uppermost in your mind when something threatens to overrun your boundaries.

- Speak up when people go too far. Cut off or suspend ties with people who persist in pushing past what you've decided is right for you.

- Remove yourself physically and emotionally from the scene if need be.

The principles of boundaries are described in depth in *Better Boundaries* by Jan Black and Greg Enns, a terrific book that can help you strengthen your boundaries with tools ranging from simple, practical techniques to a reassessment of your core beliefs about yourself.

38. Make Over Your Social Life

If you're like most of us, you have plenty of room to simplify your social life. You may find you fall prey to the desire for bigger and better entertainment to go along with all the other bigger and better stuff. More excitement, more action, more luxury—but is it what you really want? See if you can envision a less expensive, more satisfying social life for yourself in any of these stories (or the ideas for time-saving activities in #33, Mix It Up).

Jill and Hillary had been best friends since college. As relationships and work cut into their hanging-out time, they started hitting the local clothing boutiques together on Sunday afternoons. It was good to have a chance to talk about the previous week before gearing up for the next one. They didn't make these dates because they really wanted to shop; they just wanted to spend time together. The conversation was nonstop, but unfortunately the spending headed in the same direction as, without really intending to, they encouraged each other to buy. So they set a new rule—they stopped carrying money and credit cards. And eventually they stopped going into the stores at all. They walked and talked, and got much more enjoyment out of it, plus some exercise to boot. Eventually they stopped walking through the shopping district at all, instead heading for the hills.

Game night at Holly's house started as a reaction to her group's habit of meeting for overpriced cocktails at the local bar. Although she was a bit nervous suggesting the change of venue that first time, it immediately became clear that she had a hit on her hands. An art-auction board game that got the crowd going, Old Maid, good old Monopoly—it was amazing how folks went nuts for games they hadn't thought about since childhood.

Potluck dinners were the solution to Jeff's dining-out woes. When he switched to a new company and a more fulfilling job, he was determined not to lose touch with all the great friends he had made during the five years at his old firm. But constantly going out to lunch and dinner with his buddies was taking a toll on his wallet *and* his waistline (both with serious detriment to his self-image). The first time he suggested a potluck dinner at his house, he caught a bit of grief: "But I don't know how to cook!"

"But the waiters at Giovanni's really need the tips!" "You mean you expect me to *shop* for food?" Setting it up for a trial run took all the goodwill he had—and his assurance that criticizing anyone's cooking (or ordering-in) skills was strictly verboten. Not surprisingly, the closet gourmets blossomed, and the culinarophobes managed to put together a green salad here and rustle up a pie from the local bakery there. To give everyone a break now and then, they all took turns being the "bring CDs, forget the food" person. Before Jeff knew it, his popularity as a host had spread, and former coworkers who hadn't seemed to miss him too much before suddenly started sending him e-mails at his new office, hinting around about a certain do-it-yourself supper....

For those times when nothing but going out would do, Lynn and Karl switched from regular dinners out to dates at a new tea bar about a mile from their home. Carrying nothing but a couple of books and a couple of bucks, they'd walk over to the tea bar after a home-cooked meal and spend an hour or two reading, sipping, and chatting.

In addition to creatively downsizing specific activities as these folks did, consider whether you need to downsize your social life in another way. Are there people you see and activities you pursue merely out of obligation (see #32, Survey Your Tribe)? If so, be true to yourself and gently phase them out of your life. It's tough to resist things you feel you "should" do, but if you persist, you'll be rewarded with more time to spend on the pursuits and people that matter most to you.

39. Do unto Others

According to most of the major religious systems, practicing compassion and working in the service of others are among the highest pursuits. Yet these are aspects of life that many of us neglect. Okay, okay, we know what you're about to ask: how is service going to simplify my life? It may not, but learning empathy and compassion for others will improve your perspective so that these hectic parts of your life don't bother you so much. Learning to see the world through someone else's eyes may also improve your relationships. Doing service for others is pleasurable in itself, which is a hallmark of the simple life. And you get that pleasure by giving something away rather than buying something.

This is an exercise in changing your mindset. The idea is that recognizing the benefits of your complicated life can be just as valuable as making that life a little less complicated. When you recognize the good parts of your life and appreciate them, you step away from that beleaguered, put-upon state of mind that drove you to simplify in the first place. And when you combine this appreciation with the practical suggestions for making your life simpler, it really packs a punch.

Start by expanding the way you look at the world around you. It's hard to surrender your beliefs and see the world through someone else's eyes, but it's a worthwhile experience. It can happen on two levels.

First, try the larger perspective. Study other cultures, especially poor ones. Expand your awareness of limited global resources, realizing how vastly out of proportion our consumption is in the worldwide scheme. Count your blessings instead of your deficits.

As you struggle with the "burden" of having too much, visualize the thoughts and feelings of someone who has too little. Many of us have fears about becoming destitute, but they are fleeting. What if those fears were a lifelong reality? How would you feel? You might experience two different reactions to this exercise: gratitude that you have enough, and a new appreciation of what "enough" really is. So much of what we consider necessary is really just gravy, and imagining yourself in a situation where you truly don't have enough food or shelter can clarify that.

Second, stay in the compassionate mindset and direct it closer to home. Tune in to the people around you, and make a conscious effort to avoid negative thoughts and judgments about them. This will considerably smooth out your interactions with friends, coworkers, and everyone else you come into contact with. Those closest to you have fears and needs that you may not have thought about. They can certainly benefit from your compassion and attention.

Moving slightly away from your circle, there are people in your community who lack even basic necessities. Why not translate the compassion you feel for the poor and sick around the world into helping the needy in your community? Thinking this way can make many of your personal concerns seem much less weighty, perhaps even petty. For example, wouldn't you prefer disorganized kitchen cupboards stuffed with a month's worth of ingredients to a small sack of rice and no stove on which to cook it? Isn't an exhausting social life still more appealing than a lonely, isolated existence?

Acting on your highest impulses can turn even the simplest exchanges between you and other people into something sublime.

40. Pay Attention to Your Partner

The typical couple has room to simplify their relationship, whether they realize it or not. Both the practical and emotional aspects of a relationship may need attention. Many of us have habitual patterns of relating that don't serve us well and would be better off broken. Other times we end up focusing our energies on material concerns, because building a shared life in our culture is so often based on the pursuit and collection of consumer goods.

Here are a few things to try that can not only keep you on the simple track, but also help strengthen your relationship:

- Focus on your partner daily. Tune out distractions and give all your attention to this person for at least a little while. Although it's normal to think about the details of daily life, if you always have a running commentary going in your head about chores or work or the kids, then the time you spend with your partner won't be fulfilling for either of you. Remember how you felt in those early days, when you hung on each other's every word and really cared about getting to know each other? You can recapture that feeling with a little mindful interaction. (See #49, Live Mindfully, for pointers on mindfulness.)

- Give your spouse feedback about what's going on with you. Don't assume he or she can read your mind. Share in the same way you'd like him or her to share with you.

- Consider this tough question: how much of your relationship with your spouse or partner is consumed with consumption? A related question that may have come up as you've worked through this book is whether the two of you agree on the level of materialism that's appropriate in your household. If not, it'll be tough for you to get the results you want from simplifying your life. Can you find a middle ground?

- Be honest with each other about areas of your relationship that aren't satisfying, then resolve to work on them together. When there are so many outside influences that complicate your life, why let your closest relationship stay cluttered up with old issues, regrets, or seething resentments?

- Spend time together fantasizing about your dream jobs and your dream life. Where would you go, what would you do? This exercise reveals a lot about who you both are and what you value. It will also give you clues as to what to pay attention to together in your simplifying efforts.

- Start a mini reading group. Either take turns reading chapters of a book aloud to each other, or read the same book simultaneously and talk about it every chapter or two.

- If your time together is mostly taken up with shopping and buying stuff, consider whether you can spend time doing more personal things instead—things that are about the two of you, not about stuff, and that promote conversations about your inner worlds, not the outer one. Focus on each other as people, not as fellow consumers.

- Plant trees or a garden together. Better than some new furniture is a tree whose age will mirror that of your commitment.

SPIRIT SPIRIT SPIRIT SPIRIT **spirit** SPIRIT SPIRIT
SPIRIT SPIRIT SPIRIT SPIRIT SPIRIT SPIRIT SPIRIT SPIRIT
SPIRIT SPIRIT SPIRIT SPIRIT SPIRIT SPIRIT SPIRIT SPIRIT
SPIRIT SPIRIT SPIRIT SPIRIT SPIRIT SPIRIT

41. Spend Time with Yourself

Here's a basic practice that many of us neglect, even though it's crucial to the simplification process: find some "alone time" every day. If you haven't been doing this already, you're probably finding it hard to make over your life in a simpler direction. This is because we often let the needs and demands of others—or at least our reaction to those needs and demands—take over our interior landscape. The very nature of social interactions, even the most comfortable ones, is that we put energy into presenting ourselves and reacting to others. This is energy that we then can't use to shape our own, simpler lives.

Even if you avoid the trap of letting others' desires drive your life, constant companionship can make it hard to stay in touch with your own needs. Think about how physical clutter can make you feel: everything you see reminds you of something to do, someone to call, a deadline that's looming. Your thoughts become as jumbled as your environment, and you seek a remedy—perhaps you purge your closet of clutter or reorganize your drawers to restore a sense of calm. Continuous input from others can have a similar effect, to the point where your own inner voice is obscured. When that voice of truth gets drowned out, you lose sight of what's important to you, and any efforts toward rebalancing your life will likely be unsatisfying. The solution: spend time alone, and recapture your perspective on your deepest needs.

What to do in this alone time? There are countless choices. Here are just a few options:

- Sit or lie down quietly in a darkened room for fifteen minutes. Once you're settled, begin to breathe deeply. Chances are you haven't been doing it much, and you'll quickly realize that oxygen is a mind-altering substance. Let your thoughts go where they will. Don't dwell on your lengthy to-do list or begrudge yourself this small time-out.

- Meditate. Try a walking meditation. Choose a safe spot where you don't have to look out for cars. Focus on the action required to move the parts of your body and on the feel of your feet on the ground. You can do the same small loop repeatedly. Always keep in mind that it's about the walking itself, not about getting somewhere.

- Exercise. If you're not in shape, start slowly, with a walk around the block. You want to breathe easily enough to carry on a conversation, not gasp for air.

- Write in a journal. The subject is up to you: reactions to the events of your day, goals for the future, descriptions of your stressors. No one will read this but you, so let go and express your true thoughts. Give up your perfectionistic ideas about whether your writing is "good enough."

- Listen to your favorite music the way you did when you were a teenager. That means you're not simultaneously washing the dishes or doing paperwork. You're just listening.

- Do something alone that you normally do with others, and do it your way. Watch a movie none of your friends want to see. Choose the hiking route that your buddies think is too hilly, and charge right up it. Eat whatever you want, regardless of whether your usual dining partners would consider it a "real" meal. When you're on your own, you don't have to consult or compromise—it's all about you. Enjoy the opportunity to make unfettered decisions without worrying about the needs or wants of your friends and family.

42. Create an Acronym All Your Own

Remember Dave from earlier in the book? He is a regular GFM—good family man— busy with his kids' soccer and boy scouts, keeping the environment clean, paying his taxes, writing work memos on the weekend, fixing the van and the lawn mower. But what about Dave the poet? Dave the dreamer, the athlete, the intellectual?

And you haven't met her yet, but what about Karen, Dave's wife? She's just as wrapped up in potlucks, chauffeur duty, and her own job selling real estate. What about Karen the potter? What about Karen the political activist, the genealogist, the sex kitten?

When you run your life like a business, with appointments and prioritized schedules, you run the risk of starving your soul. You may be too efficient to budget time for such tasks as smelling the roses, meditating on the meaning of life, writing a love poem, becoming a vegetarian, doing yoga exercises, contributing to charity, or staying in better touch with your brothers and sisters.

These kinds of ongoing personal practices don't mesh well with the more mundane demands of a busy life. You feel a little stupid putting "meditate" or "be more positive" on your to-do list every day, especially if you continually give these items such low priority that they are almost never accomplished.

One solution is to devise an acronym all your own. Dave's acronym is "CREW," which stands for:

Create

Read

Exercise

Write

In the upper left-hand corner of each day's schedule, Dave writes "CREW." Before he goes to bed each night he underlines the C for "create" if he has done any work on a poem that day. He underlines the R if he has read in a good book and the

E if he went jogging or to the gym. If he had a dream the night before that he wrote down in his dream journal, he underlines the W.

When Dave is feeling stale and depressed, he looks back over the last few days and, sure enough, he finds that hardly any of the CREWs are underlined. He knows he hasn't been feeding his soul enough. Sometimes at the end of a busy, frustrating day, he is cheered up by underlining just one letter.

Karen's acronym is "PAGES," which stands for:

<u>P</u>olitics

<u>A</u>rt

<u>G</u>enealogy

<u>E</u>at healthy

<u>S</u>ex

In the daily diary she keeps by her bedside, she underlines the P if she has written a letter for Amnesty International or gone to a neighborhood meeting. If she has worked on her pottery or her family tree, she underlines the A for "art" or the G for "genealogy." She underlines the E if she ate a reasonable amount of healthy food that day. She gets an S for "sex" if she went to bed early, showered and put on perfume before bed, wore a lacy nightgown, or did something else to keep her and Dave's sex life lively.

What would your acronym be? Write down all the things you want to do or become, the things that you seldom get around to, and pare the list down to the four or five most cherished items. Brainstorm some synonyms for these items and see what you can come up with in the way of an acronym. It should be short, simple, and easy to remember. Use your acronym as a subtle reminder to feed your soul, expand your horizons, express yourself, and help others.

43. Exercise Your Breath, Heart, and Mind

Most of us have heard all we want to hear about why we "should" be exercising—from our spouses, kids, friends, doctors, and the media. Why then do so many of us ignore that advice, shrugging off what we hear about the benefits for our cardiovascular system, bones, and muscles? Why isn't everybody clued in to the mood-boosting effects, the clarity of mind, the meditative state that exercise brings? Probably it's because with everything else going on in our lives, including all the things we do for other people—all the things we do because we "should"—the barriers can seem insurmountable, and exercise can seem like just another "should" on a very long list.

Since you're reading this book, you may be thinking "How can *adding* an activity to my already busy life possibly make things simpler?" Well, it all boils down to the feeling of your body in motion, your breath deepening, your heart pounding, your mind free of distractions. This is as simple as it gets. Even if you set aside its physical benefits and its longer-term emotional and coping benefits, exercise is worth doing for the momentary joy of it. And joy, that pure emotion, is a key part of the simple life—just ask any small child turning cartwheels, or the next dog you see racing down the sidewalk with its tongue flopping wildly. Why toss such an opportunity for joy aside?

Let's say then that the benefits of exercise are a given, and talk instead about how you can hop over the barriers and into a new frame of mind about exercise. Todd is a good example of the "where do I find the time?" type. As a sporting goods sales rep, he's on the road constantly, under high pressure from the company he represents and from his clients. Surrounded by sports equipment—and sports-crazed people—all day, he began to feel odd about having so much trouble taking time for exercise. So Todd decided that if he had to practically live out of his car, he'd do it his way. So among the sample cases in his van, he squeezed in several survival kits: swimsuit, goggles, cap, and towel; running shoes, shorts, and T-shirt; a jump rope; flexible bands to use for toning and stretching; and walking shoes for days when he didn't have time to change into special gear. Now when he drives by a pool or a running track while making his rounds, he can hop out and work out. And when he has to spend the night out of town, he doesn't have to skip his exercise.

Jennifer, on the other hand, is the "I hate to exercise" sort. Or at least she used to be. In elementary school, she played basketball, but she really wasn't very good at it and didn't enjoy it. In high school, she joined the track and field team, but never found her niche. For a few years, she fell into the trap of thinking she just wasn't cut out for physical activity of any kind. Shortly after college graduation, as Jennifer embarked on a new job, a friend coaxed her into trying a modern dance class. The music, the creative expression, the sweat: Jennifer couldn't believe that she could enjoy physical activity so much. Finally she understood that it was all a matter of finding the right activity. A few years later, she added weekend hikes to her schedule so she could spend more time outdoors. This time, she invited an exercise-phobic friend to join her, and turned him on to the benefits of fitness as well.

What type are you? Do you fit one of these profiles, or do you have other barriers to exercise? If you're a single parent with kids, a very overweight person with health fears, or an older person who's never followed an exercise program, then ask for help when you need it. If you have health concerns, by all means check with your doctor before you start to exercise. If you have motivational or time-management issues, request help and advice from friends and family members who make exercise a part of their lives. A supportive environment is key to making major behavioral changes.

44. Feed Your Soul

We admit it: simplifying your diet may seem pretty tough. Because when it comes to food, we're conditioned to think that the simplest thing is to eat what's there—the convenient stuff. Unfortunately, what that too often means in our society these days is highly processed "food" that bears little resemblance to its original form. It's obvious that this type of food is complicated stuff.

But what if you looked at food according to what your *body* sees as simple? There's plenty of food out there that's reasonably close to its natural state, not some unrecognizable mishmash that's dyed, extruded, fried, or filled with enough preservatives to make it last just about forever. By appreciating good food, eating mindfully, and recognizing your emotional links with food, you can take giant steps toward simple nourishment. (Saving time in a simplified kitchen is the subject of #11, Change Your Culinary Attitude—check it out.)

So how do you appreciate good food in its natural state? Start by recognizing that what you take in provides the building blocks of your body. It seems fair to say that the growth and repair of your tissues is a subject that deserves respect. Yet you may give more attention to what you put in your car's gas tank than what you put in your mouth. (Hey, it's not logical, but it's common.) It's pretty amazing that your body can extract all the nutrients it needs from the foods you put in it. Try to help it along by eating a wide variety of lightly processed foods, including as many fresh vegetables and fruits as possible. Another approach to appreciating your food is to think about where it comes from. Who grew it or raised it, and under what conditions? How did the food get to you? Once you think about it, you'll realize that the abundance we enjoy today is something to be thankful for.

Mindful eating is a great tool that will help you make the shift from gobbling your food to really enjoying it. (It's also a stress-busting, relaxing experience.) It's best to do this exercise when you're at least a little bit hungry. Choose a tasty food that's good for you; a piece of fruit is an excellent choice. Set aside some uninterrupted time and clear away all distractions—you can't be mindful while reading or watching television.

First, observe the food. Really *look* at it. Feel it. Smell it. Notice your reactions to all these sensory perceptions. Does your mouth start to water a bit? Does your stomach rumble? Are you reminded of past experiences with this food? Now take your first bite. Notice the texture and taste of the food, as well as any sound it makes when you bite it. Begin to chew, and notice how the taste develops in your mouth. Pay attention to the act of chewing, and chew very thoroughly. Swallow, and notice this process as well. Picture the food moving down your throat and into your stomach. Don't reach for the next bite until you're completely finished with the first. Continue to eat, paying attention to all of your senses and to your whole body's reaction. Can you feel your hunger abating? Do you feel energized?

Another valuable dietary habit is to tune into your emotional links with food. Do you overeat to stuff your feelings down? Do you pound caffeine and gobble sugar when you're stressed so you can keep go-go-going despite your body's signals? Do you stop eating entirely when you're nervous? In addition to being a way for us to deal with our emotions, food can also inspire feelings in us. Unfortunately, these are often negative, socially induced feelings of guilt and furtiveness. It can be hard to let go of this range of tangled emotions and just see food for what it is: nourishment for our bodies that is also a source of pleasure and a catalyst for social interaction. Make it your goal to separate your emotional ups and downs from your eating habits. Remind yourself that you *can* create a balanced diet that allows for both health and enjoyment. It's possible to deal with stresses in ways that don't wreak havoc on your body through stuffing or starving. Food is one of the simplest pleasures in life. Respect your body by giving it the best, and do it with relish!

45. Take a Daily Constitutional

How often do you go out and walk just for the sake of walking? We're not talking about that walk you take after Thanksgiving dinner, since its main purpose is to get your food to settle down enough so you can eat another piece of pie. And last week when you walked instead of driving to the store because your car was in the shop? That's not what we have in mind either. A daily constitutional is a walk you take for the pure pleasure of it, because it feels good to step out the door with nothing but the house key in your pocket, your arms swinging free, your eyes ready to see what the neighborhood has to offer. And it's not meant to be exercise, so don't put yourself under pressure to work up a sweat and get your heart rate up. Those walks are great too, in a different way. The daily constitutional is all about relaxation and ritual.

Ashley's favorite walk is a treasured break after a stressful day at work. It takes her on a three-mile route where she can visit five friendly cats to whom she has given names that their owners might not approve ("Hello, Mr. Fluffy Pants!"). The walk also provides her with a snapshot of the neighborhood she's lived in and loved for years. There's the neighbor who always reads his new library book as he walks the dog. Her friend Kevin and his dog, Moose, run down the other side of the street with a wave and a bark. Hey, they're finally renovating that pink house—just in time, as it would have crumbled to the ground pretty soon. Students whiz by on bikes on their way home from the university, Frisbee players frolic in the park—it's all there, and it's all comforting and familiar.

But there's no need to commit to three miles. How about just a couple of blocks instead? Gus, who lives in a bustling urban neighborhood, takes his walk every morning as soon as he awakens, before his shower-and-coffee routine. He puts on sweats and a cap (to cover up his bed-head hairdo). As soon as he steps outside, he sees the welcome sight of the local shop owners rolling up their awnings as the delivery trucks arrive with the day's fresh produce. The woman who owns the Japanese import store is out sweeping the sidewalk, and the earliest of his early-bird neighbors are already sprinting to the train station. He stops to talk to the couple next door, who are just returning from the first walk of several they will take with their two miniature poodles. Seeing them all enjoying their walk almost makes up for the times he hears them yapping (the poodles, not the neighbors) through the walls of the apartment building.

Stephanie's only time for a daily walk is after dark, when she doesn't feel comfortable going out by herself. So she takes her boyfriend, but they have a rule that talking while walking is strictly optional. During their twenty-minute stroll, they often find themselves looking up at the stars without saying much at all. But they return home feeling more in touch with themselves, the night air, and each other.

Start your daily-walk ritual today, and see what *you* can see.

46. Enter the White Hole

Try this sanity-saving mind game when you are feeling overwhelmed by all the "stuff" in your life: body stuff like aging and illness, head stuff like classes and reports, heart stuff like divorce and kids, wallet stuff like bills and taxes, spirit stuff like death and guilt, and just plain stuff stuff like storm windows and fabric remnants.

The accumulated pressure of stuff can weigh you down until you feel like you're at the bottom of a black hole, a collapsed star whose gravity is so strong that even light can't escape it. At the bottom of a black hole of stuff, you feel suffocated, confined, and blinded. Your personal space is compressed to zero. You handle one crisis after another, pushing them away for a little while until they come crashing back down on you. That's when you need to enter the white hole.

For the best results, lie down in a quiet place and close your eyes to do this, at least for the first try. Later you can do it while riding on the bus or waiting in line at the grocery. Close your eyes and relax. Imagine that you're surrounded by all the dense, heavy stuff of your life, pressing in on you so you can't move or breathe. Imagine that at the center of your chest there is a tiny white seed, like a pearl. This is the seed of the white hole. The white hole is what you get when you turn a black hole inside out: antigravity, emptiness, total lack of stuff. Nothing sticks to it. Nothing can get inside it.

In your mind's eye, expand the sphere of emptiness outward from your chest until it surrounds you. As it expands, it pushes all your life stuff away, shielding you from the stuff's weight. Feel the pressure of responsibilities, deadlines, and worries lift away.

Then let the white hole continue to expand into your immediate surroundings, pushing away all the stuff and people and connections and obligations and habits in your life. Let the sphere expand to a comfortable size, big enough to give you some temporary distance from all the stuff in your life—a few yards in diameter, a mile, a light year, whatever you need.

Enjoy the space and the feeling of lightness for a while. If thoughts about your problems or interests come up, imagine them hitting the outside of the pearly shell and sliding off. If your mental image of the white hole falters, recreate it smaller and expand it again.

When you are ready, imagine that you have control of the boundary between the white hole and all your stuff. You can relax the antigravity effect in certain spots so that some chosen stuff can drift back into your space. You can decide what to let back in, how fast it comes in, and how closely to let it approach you.

Now, what would you let back into your life first? What would you let back in second? One by one, let different relationships, possessions, activities, habits, and so on back into the sphere, until they comprise all the stuff you really want in your life. Compare how much stuff is outside the sphere to the amount of stuff inside the sphere.

Tell yourself, "I live inside the white hole. It's a special place, as sparse and quiet or as full and busy as I want it to be. This inner sanctum is available to me any time I want to enter it."

47. Explore Your Creative Side

Creative pursuits aren't just a pleasant way to while away your free moments. They're an expression of your truest self and even a route to fulfillment. Making time for art—and in particular, giving yourself the freedom to create whatever feels right to you—can help you know yourself better and put your emotional and physical needs into perspective.

Pablo Picasso said, "Art is the elimination of the unnecessary." This statement expresses how art connects you to the basic root of who you are. It further suggests the idea that how you live your life, and how you experience and enjoy it, can be creative acts. Picasso's words also happen to express the very essence of simplifying.

When you get in touch with your creative self, you can separate out yourself and your needs from all the demands and requests you hear from family, friends, and society. Whether they're implicitly demanded or explicitly requested, these things we do for or because of others can build up slowly over time and obscure the essence of who we are. How to stay in touch? It's simple: do something artful every day. Write a paragraph or one line of a poem. Tickle the ivories. Capture a mood or a facial expression with a few strokes of a brush. Cultivate flowers in a pot on the front porch. However small, each effort nourishes your creative core and keeps you in touch with the opinions and feelings that really count in your life: yours.

Although we may not realize it's true, our thirst for consumption can mask our creative urges. Art can be a way to find fulfillment by creating rather than consuming. Katherine, a publishing executive, had loved the visual arts for as long as she could remember. Growing up with a volatile, emotionally overwrought mother, she relished drawing and collage as an escape and an outlet for her own fears and frustrations. Later, in college, painting became a near-obsession during a breakup from a controlling boyfriend. But because she'd never given herself much credit for her artistic talents, her painting and drawing quickly fell by the wayside once she settled into married life and had two sons. As Katherine worked her way up in her field, she found it even harder to justify carving out a place in her schedule for that "messing around" she used to do with such fervor.

One thing she did find plenty of time for was shopping. Intoxicated by the color combinations she could create, she jumped into home decorating with both feet. But as soon as she finished filling one room with new furniture, she'd immediately move to the next without pausing to admire her work or to question why she was so driven to remake her environment. Even though each completed room was more striking than the last, nothing ever seemed good enough. Another style always came into fashion, and she figured this one would be just right. Even her wardrobe was a sea of color—she bought clothes she'd never, ever dream of wearing, all for the sake of seeing them stacked up in her perfectly organized closets.

As she redid her home office for the third time, she came across a large portfolio full of watercolors she'd done in college, and nearly passed out from shock. Here was what she'd been trying to capture for the last ten years. It was suddenly obvious to her that she had filed away these true expressions, diverted into thinking they weren't important, and had instead focused on redoing the surface of her life over and over. No surprise that she'd been feeling unfulfilled for a good many years! In her case, the solution was simple—she devoted the attention she'd paid to surface style to exploring her creative soul instead.

If you shop to fill a creative urge, you can do the same thing. Recognize that your desire to consume may come from your desire for creative fulfillment. Pick up a notebook and pen and write something, or make your next shopping trip a jaunt to the art store for a sampling of pastels or paints.

48. Use the Mr. Coffee Mantra

Simplifying your life often involves forming new habits, such as daily relaxation, regular exercise, spiritual practices (such as prayer or meditation), noticing and enjoying simple pleasures, or just taking a quiet moment for yourself each day. These changes are simple and don't take much time, but they can be difficult to incorporate into a busy life.

The way to make these new habits stick is to tie them to a regular habit you already have. For example, Louise was a corporate trainer who frequently recommended the calming, centering effects of meditation, but was much too busy to practice it herself. She would fall into bed after midnight, once again having failed to practice her daily meditation, feeling like a hypocrite and a fool.

Louise was saved by her coffee maker. "Mr. Coffee is my guru," she now says. "He gave me my mantra and guides my meditation every morning." Her favorite type of meditation was mantra meditation, in which you focus exclusively on a sight or sound, and refocus when your mind wanders. She found it to be an easy, relaxing form of meditation that she could combine with her unvarying habit of making coffee first thing in the morning.

She would set up the coffee machine, toss a couch cushion on the floor near the kitchen door, hit the switch on the machine, and sit cross-legged on the cushion. She closed her eyes and meditated on the sound of the coffee machine.

It was a perfect mantra. The sounds were just interesting enough to keep her attention. They took exactly 5.5 minutes from start to finish, changing slightly over time, so she always knew about how long she had to go and when to stop. There were three distinct sounds. First, the heating element made a ratcheting sound like a roller coaster being cranked uphill. Then there was a gurgling, gassy sound as heated water expanded and made it "over the hump" and into the filter area. These two sounds repeated over and over, subtly masking and revealing the third sound of the brewed coffee trickling into the pot, which started as an almost imperceptible drip-drip-drip, built to a steady babble, then died away to drips again at the end.

Louise named each sound as she heard it, and synchronized her breathing to the mantra's recurring rhythm: "Ratcheting … gurgling … trickling … ratcheting … gurgling … trickling."

Toward the end, the ratcheting and trickling quieted and the gurgling stretched out into a long sigh, then went silent. She ended her meditation with her own long sigh, rose, and poured a steaming cup of coffee as a reward for having done her morning spiritual practice.

You can use any routine habit to anchor a new one. If you've been wanting to relieve tension regularly, try straightening your shoulders and taking a deep breath every time you answer the phone. Let feeding the dog be the reminder to take your vitamins. Every time you go to the bathroom, ask yourself, "What have I done so far today to reach my goals of a simpler life?" When you pick up the mail, stop and pull one weed out of the front yard and remind yourself of your commitment to get closer to nature. If you have a regular long commute, replace the chatter of the radio with musical, instructional, or inspirational tapes. Do your favorite yoga pose while your computer is booting.

49. Live Mindfully

Slowing down and practicing mindfulness will help you recognize and appreciate the simple things in life. What could be more fulfilling than letting go of mental clutter and enjoying the little things? Follow these basic precepts to set yourself on the road to mindful living:

- Pay attention.

- Be relaxed.

- Enjoy what you do.

At first, you might think you're already living this way. But then you recall your habit of suddenly snapping into consciousness while driving, with no memory of having navigated the previous several miles, stop signs and all. Or you turn the page of your book, only to realize that you have no idea what you've just read. Maybe you've found yourself standing in front of an open kitchen drawer with no concept of what you are looking for. And there's the old familiar feeling of confusion when the person you've just phoned picks up the line, and you realize you have no idea whose number you dialed.

Instances like these demonstrate how often we put our minds on automatic pilot. They're an understandable reaction to a feeling of being overwhelmed and having too much to do. Mindfulness is a great simplifying tool, because it's an antidote to doing too much.

So how can you actually *be* mindful instead of mindless? There's just one step to this technique: stay in the moment, and be conscious of what you are doing. There are also a couple of things *not* to do: don't think ahead or look back, and don't do something just for the purpose of getting through it. When we look ahead constantly, we not only rush through the less pleasant tasks, we also tend to hurry through the things we love to do, because we're always thinking or worrying about what to do next. Thich Nhat Hanh expresses this concept beautifully in *The Miracle of Mindfulness*: "If while washing dishes, we think only of the cup of tea that awaits us ... then we are not 'washing the dishes to wash the dishes.' What's more, we are not alive during the time we are washing the dishes…. If we can't wash the dishes, the chances are we won't be able to drink our tea either."

A good way to practice being mindful is to follow your breath. This doesn't require any special training or mysterious techniques. But if you're like most people, you rarely do it, because breathing just happens automatically, right? (Except for those times you catch yourself holding your breath out of nervousness or stress. We hope simplifying is helping you reduce the number of these instances.) To breathe mindfully, simply take notice of your breaths and try to make them as calm and even as possible. Your breaths should be long and slow, and should come from your diaphragm rather than your upper chest. Pay attention to each breath, letting other thoughts fall away and disappear. You can do this exercise any time you think of it.

Make it a goal to be mindful in general, but also set aside short periods in which to practice. This will improve your chances of making mindfulness a habit. Once you've practiced with breathing, try it with other things: walking, eating, doing chores. As you learn to live this way, you'll feel more centered, and you'll gain an appreciation for your body's abilities and its most basic needs.

Mindfulness can even help you deal with the tricky parts of life that just can't be simplified. Julia Cameron described how her grandmother got through trying times "by standing knee-deep in the flow of life and paying close attention." In her case, paying attention to the seasons and natural life around her was a saving grace in times of financial trouble. You might use mindfulness to improve your work life or to enjoy your time alone.

In the simplifying spirit of doing less but doing it better, an old Zen saying is especially appropriate: "How you do anything is how you do everything."

50. Reframe It, Rethink It

Perhaps there are some areas of your life that just can't be simplified in the ways we've been talking about here. Making a living, raising a family, dealing with illness—these and many other aspects of life aren't simple in nature. When you add in your unique challenges and circumstances, the result may be some stubbornly complicated areas. But don't feel bad about those spots where your simplifying efforts fail to get you the results you are seeking. Embrace them, and look at them in a new light.

Throughout this book we've focused on how you can adapt your perspective to make your life less complicated—by focusing on priorities, resisting the cultural norms that don't work for you, and taking time for yourself. You can take this practice a step further and reframe those things that can't be simplified.

Your relationship with your kids offers great opportunities to reframe complex situations. Sure, there are lots of ways to simplify your family life. You can adapt your household routines and modify your standards about housekeeping (see #8). You can adjust your schedule and theirs to allow for as much quality time together as possible (see #35). You can raise your kids to be less TV-focused and less materialistic, by setting rules and showing your good example (see #12).

But whatever you do to simplify daily life, the parent-child relationship is by nature complicated. You'll have times of conflict, possibly including wars over what level of materialism is appropriate. Even though your effort to spend lots of time with them will help build a strong relationship that just might keep things simpler during the tough teenage years and beyond, there's no guarantee of a smooth road ahead. So when you hit a rough patch with your kids, look at it as a parenting challenge. Overcoming it is the work you're uniquely qualified to do, and it's the kind of challenge that is the opposite of pointless, because the payoff is so big.

Think about all the areas where reframing can help: a scary new project at work plants the seed for a skill set that could lead you to a new career. An illness in the family is a wake-up call to take better care of each other and spend more time together. Trouble in a long-standing friendship can be interpreted as a sign of growth and change on your part—or the other person's.

With the right attitude, you can reframe difficult situations into positive challenges that can lead you to new accomplishments. That's why it's worthwhile to design your life to be as close to your simple ideal as possible. The point is, even though you can't simplify everything, your success in some areas makes dealing with inevitable complications in other parts of your life that much easier.

By changing the way you look at stressors, and adapting your responses to them, you can gain the benefits of simplifying despite those resistant areas. A great many aspects of life can't be controlled, however hard we try—and some of these are what make life exciting and challenging. So if a practical change isn't feasible, try a mental one instead.

further reading

FURTHER READING FURTHER READING

FURTHER READING FURTHER READING FURTHER READING

FURTHER READING FURTHER READING FURTHER READING

FURTHER READING FURTHER READING

Black, Jan, and Greg Enns. 1997. *Better Boundaries: Owning and Treasuring Your Life.* Oakland, Calif.: New Harbinger Publications.

Callenbach, Ernest. 2000. *Living Cheaply with Style: Live Better and Spend Less.* Second edition. Berkeley, Calif.: Ronin Publishing.

Cameron, Julia. 1992. *The Artist's Way: A Spiritual Path to Higher Creativity.* New York: J.P. Tarcher.

Dacyzyn, Amy. 1999. *The Complete Tightwad Gazette: Promoting Thrift as a Viable Alternative Lifestyle.* New York: Random House.

Dominguez, Joe, and Vicki Robin. 1999. *Your Money or Your Life.* New edition. New York: Penguin.

Eisenson, Marc, Gerri Detweiler, and Nancy Castleman. *Stop Junk Mail Forever.* Elizaville, N.Y.: Good Advice Press. Call (800) 255-0899 or visit www.goodadvicepress.com.

Elgin, Duane. 1993. *Voluntary Simplicity: Toward a Way of Life That Is Outwardly Simple, Inwardly Rich.* Revised edition. New York: Quill.

Hanh, Thich Nhat. 1976. *The Miracle of Mindfulness.* Boston: Beacon Press.

McKay, Matthew, and Patrick Fanning. 1991. *Prisoners of Belief: Exposing and Changing Beliefs That Control Your Life.* Oakland, Calif.: New Harbinger Publications.

Schor, Juliet. 1999. *The Overspent American: Why We Want What We Don't Need.* New York: HarperCollins.

 **Patrick Fanning** is the coauthor of nine popular self-help books, including *The Daily Relaxer* and the *Self-Esteem Companion*. He pursues his passions for painting and writing from his home studio in Graton, California, where he lives simply with his wife and son.

Heather Garnos Mitchener, a freelance writer and editor, changed jobs to find a more balanced way of life. She resides with her husband in the San Francisco Bay Area.

Some Other New Harbinger Titles

The 50 Best Ways to Simplify Your Life, Item FWSL $11.95

When Anger Hurts Your Relationship, Item WARY $13.95

The Couple's Survival Workbook, Item CPSU $18.95

Loving Your Teenage Daughter, Item LYTD $14.95

The Hidden Feeling of Motherhood, Item HFM $14.95

Parenting Well When Your Depressed, Item PWWY $17.95

Thinking Pregnant, Item TKPG $13.95

Pregnancy Stories, Item PS $14.95

The Co-Parenting Survival Guide, Item CPSG $14.95

Family Guide to Emotional Wellness, Item FGEW $24.95

How to Survive and Thrive in an Empty Nest, Item NEST $13.95

Children of the Self-Absorbed, Item CSAB $14.95

The Adoption Reunion Survival Guide, Item ARSG $13.95

Undefended Love, Item UNLO $13.95

Why Can't I Be the Parent I Want to Be?, Item PRNT $12.95

Kid Cooperation, Item COOP $14.95

Breathing Room: Creating Space to Be a Couple, Item BR $14.95

Why Children Misbehave and What to do About it, Item BEHV $14.95

Couple Skills, Item SKIL $15.95

The Power of Two, Item PWR $15.95

The Queer Parent's Primer, Item QPPM $14.95

Call **toll free, 1-800-748-6273,** or log on to our online bookstore at **www.newharbinger.com** to order. Have your Visa or Mastercard number ready. Or send a check for the titles you want to New Harbinger Publications, Inc., 5674 Shattuck Ave., Oakland, CA 94609. Include $4.50 for the first book and 75¢ for each additional book, to cover shipping and handling. (California residents please include appropriate sales tax.) Allow two to five weeks for delivery.

Prices subject to change without notice.